FLASHBACKS

THE FLASHBACKS SERIES IS SPONSORED BY THE
EUROPEAN ETHNOLOGICAL RESEARCH CENTRE
CELTIC & SCOTTISH STUDIES
UNIVERSITY OF EDINBURGH
27–29 GEORGE STREET
EDINBURGH EH8 9LD

FLASHBACKS

OTHER TITLES IN THE SERIES:

The Making of *Am Fasgadh*
An Account of the Origins of the Highland Folk Museum by its Founder

Isabel Frances Grant MBE, LLD

From Kelso to Kalamazoo
The Life and Times of George Taylor

Edited by Margaret Jeary and Mark A. Mulhern

Showfolk
An Oral History of a Fairground Dynasty

Frank Bruce

Scotland's Land Girls
Breeches, Bombers and Backaches

Edited by Elaine M. Edwards

An Orkney Childhood
Duncan Cameron Mackenzie

| FLASHBACKS |

Galoshins Remembered

'A penny was a lot in these days'

Edited by
Emily Lyle

in association with
THE EUROPEAN ETHNOLOGICAL RESEARCH CENTRE
AND NMS ENTERPRISES LIMITED – PUBLISHING
NATIONAL MUSEUMS SCOTLAND

GENERAL EDITOR
Alexander Fenton

Published in Great Britain in 2011 by
NMS Enterprises Limited – Publishing
NMS Enterprises Limited
National Museums Scotland
Chambers Street, Edinburgh EH1 1JF

Text © National Museums Scotland
and European Ethnological Research
Centre 2011

Images: all photographs
© as credited 2011

No reproduction permitted without
written permission to the publisher in
the first instance.

ISBN 978-1-905267-56-9

*No part of this publication may
be reproduced, stored in a retrieval
system or transmitted, in any form or
by any means, electronic, mechanical,
photocopying, recording or other-
wise, without the prior permission of
the publisher.*

The right of Emily Lyle to be identified
as the author of this book has been
asserted by her in accordance with the
Copyright, Designs and Patents Act
1988.

**British Library Cataloguing in
Publication Data**
A catalogue record of this book
is available from the British Library.

Cover design by Mark Blackadder.
Cover photograph: An outdoor per-
   formance at Biggar, 1982 (*Source:*
   School of Scottish Studies Archive).
Internal text design by NMS Enter-
   prises Limited – Publishing.
Printed and bound in Great Britain
   by Bell & Bain Limited, Glasgow.

For a full listing of related titles and
the work of the EERC please visit:

www.nms.ac.uk/books   [and]
**www.celtscot.ed.ac.uk/
   EERC_home.htm**

CONTENTS

Acknowledgements 6
List of Illustrations 10
Foreword by Mark A. Mulhern 11

GALOSHINS REMEMBERED

Introduction 13
Recollections from the Players and Observers 38
  1 *James Purves – Melrose, 1897–1899* 38
  2 *William Brown – Melrose, 1912–1913* 43
  3 *Harry Fox – Morebattle, 1938–1942* 48
  4 *Michael Crosby – Hawick,*
     1950–1955 and 1991–1996 63
  5 *Wat Ramage – Westruther, 1914–1917* 70
  6 *Peter Thomson – Biggar, 1925–1928* 74
  7 *Mrs Sheila Duffy (née Harris) –*
     Muirkirk, 1933–1934 98
  8 *David Laurie and Mrs Margaret Muir*
     (née Laurie) – Kirkcowan, 1921–1925 107
  9 *David Laurie – Newton Stewart, 1926–1929* 117
 10 *David Kerr – Armadale, 1930–1932* 122
 11 *John Anderson – Falkirk, 1905–1908* 132
 12 *Robert Hendry – Camelon, 1922–1927* 145
 13 *James Wands – Dennyloanhead, 1912–1916* 161
 14 *Andrew Rennie – Kippen, 1899–1903* 175
Notes 183
Bibliography 184
Glossary 188

ACKNOWLEDGEMENTS

THE material in this book comes mainly from recordings I have made for the School of Scottish Studies Sound Archive, while some additional material has been drawn from video recordings and from correspondence. I have been happy to involve others in the sessions for recording this very lively little tradition and students and visiting scholars have often taken part with me. Sometimes, too, valuable contributions have been made by interested people living in the community where I planned to record who gave me introductions and participated in the discussion. The names of those directly involved appear in the headnotes, but others, too, offered help in a variety of ways which I warmly appreciated. Sometimes I located those who knew the play simply by knocking on doors and asking if the people who answered had any knowledge of it, but more frequently I paid a follow-up visit after a response to a published appeal.

My first fieldwork relating to the play took place in 1976–77 when I held a fellowship from the Humanities Research Centre at the Australian National University in Canberra to record Scottish oral traditions in Australia, and I began recording in Scotland in the latter part of 1977.[1] Sheffield University had been taking a special interest in the topic of folk drama throughout the British Isles, developing the work outlined in Cawte, Helm and Peacock (1967), and I linked up with scholars there and received from Paul Smith copies of all the correspondence relating to Scotland that had been gathered after appeals for information had been made in magazines. I would like to thank Paul for his continuing friendly interest over the years and also take this opportunity to thank the many others in the international community of folk drama enthusiasts with whom I have had valuable contacts, including Carsten Bregenhøj, Eddie Cass, Terry Gunnell, Brian Hayward, Neill Martin, Peter Millington, Norman Peacock and Steve Roud. At the time when I began recording memories of the play, Brian Hayward was working on Scottish folk drama at the University of Glasgow and he drew on my published material when he eventually brought out his book, *Galoshins: The Scottish Folk Play* (1992), which concentrates on giving the texts along with detailed discussion of the dramatic action and his own interpretations of the historical evidence. We agreed that it would be better to bring together the reminiscences of performers and members of the audience in a separate book, and this is what is now offered. Dr Hayward has since written a survey article,[2] but my 'Hayward' references are to his book. David Fergus, Linlithgow, who also had a keen interest in the play, kindly made an appeal on my behalf in an article he published in *The Scots Magazine* in January 1982.

I am extremely grateful for grants from The Russell Trust (1994) and The Research Fund of the Arts, Divinity and Music Faculty Group at the University of Edinburgh (1996) for transcribing *Galoshins* tapes. In many cases I have been able to base my final transcriptions published in this book on the transcriptions done by students at the University of Edinburgh. I would like to acknowledge this much appreciated help here and I list the tape transcribers and their contribution:

Brian Alexander (SA2001.025)
Audrey Bain (SA1977.205, SA1982.109–117, SA1982.137, SA1984.29–31)
John Beech (SA1979.150, SA1980.101)
Heather Holmes (SA1982.125–6)
Alyne Jones (SA1982.123–4)
Robert Lowe (SA1980.091)
Fiona Shanks (SA1977.205)

Douglas Strang (SA1984.033)
Fraser Thomson (SA1979.173)
Alison Wattie (SA1979.151, SA1980.100)

Audrey Bain and Joy Fraser also offered very welcome assistance with organising *Galoshins* materials. Students at the University of Stirling also had a heavy involvement with the play while I was lecturing in Folk Life Studies there. Karin Harrington, Tracey Heaton and Rob Watling receive mention with Andrew Rennie [14], and they and Catherine Nickolls and Gordon McCullough were present at a number of interviews. In the transcriptions offered here, omission is indicated by '…' and a broken-off sentence by '–'. Hesitations are generally not included and some repetitions are silently omitted. The characters' names given in italics with the play texts are mainly editorial.

I am very pleased to have been able to work on this play in the friendly and supportive atmosphere of my department at the University of Edinburgh, which was formerly The School of Scottish Studies and is now Celtic and Scottish Studies. I am especially grateful to my colleague, Katherine Campbell, for transcribing and preparing computerised copies of the music for this book. Archive assistance, often of a technical nature, has been invaluable over the years and I should like to express particular thanks to Caroline Milligan for cheerfully and efficiently making archive materials available to me in recent months. Other very welcome recent assistance has come from Colin Gately, Joy Katzmarzig, Cathlin Macauley, Mark A. Mulhern, Chris Robinson, Stuart Robinson, Alexandra Stegner and Lesley A. Taylor. With respect to illustration, I am indebted to Ian MacKenzie for copying the family photographs of William Brown and Wat Ramage, and to William B. Brown and Mrs Betty Ramage for providing them. R. McEwan of the University of Stirling very kindly made the video of Andrew Rennie and five Kippen boys.

And finally I should like to offer my very warm thanks to all the people who shared their memories with me. I have tried to contact those whose voices are heard in this book, but a good deal of time has gone by and I have often been unsuccessful. I would be very pleased to hear from any contributors or family members whom I have been unable to reach and to arrange for them to receive a complimentary copy of the book. Should there be any profit from this volume in the Flashback series, it would be ploughed back into the production programme to help to finance the publication of further memories of the past in Scotland.

If you have a recollection of *Galoshins* that you would like to share, it is not too late! I will be happy to hear from you with a view to placing your written or recorded memories in the School of Scottish Studies Archives for the benefit of interested people in future generations who regretfully will not have any direct access to the community tradition of the play, however much they may enjoy revivals of it.

Emily Lyle, Editor
CELTIC AND SCOTTISH STUDIES
UNIVERSITY OF EDINBURGH
EDINBURGH 2011

LIST OF ILLUSTRATIONS

1. The fight.
2. The bargaining for the cure (see also page 9).
3. Singing the blessing.
4. Setting off to the next house.
5. Wat Ramage.
6. Andrew Rennie.
7. William Brown.
8–18. An outdoor performance at Biggar ... produced by Brian Lambie in 1982.
    8. Room (Diane Ritchie); 9. Wee Yin (Lorna Clark); 10. King George (David Hodgson); 11. Turkey Snipe (Colin Moore); 12. Beelzebub (Graham Gordon); 13. Galashians (John Tweedie); 14. Tea, Toast and Butter (Felicity Gerraghty); 15. Sir William Wallace (Steven Bolton); 16. Doctor Brown (Michelle Gillespie); 17. Johnnie Funny (Jacqueline Tweedie); 18. King George and Galashians fight.
19. Room announces 'Here's two warriors come to fight' as Sir William Wallace and King George prepare for battle.
20. Doctor Brown cures King George while Sir William Wallace looks on.
21–31. Stills from a video of Andrew Rennie performing the play.
32–34. Five boys from Kippen perform the play as taught them by Andrew Rennie.
    32. The Admiral (Cameron Sharp) and Galoshins (Thomas Cassidy) fight, encouraged by Keep Silence (Craig MacDonnell); 33. Doctor Brown (Tommy Smith) enters; 34. Keekem Funny (Alan Edmiston) prepares to take the collection.

FOREWORD

THE Flashbacks series presents, in printed form, the words of individuals concerning aspects of their lives in Scotland. The content is variously composed of interview transcriptions, memoir or autobiography. The aim of the series is to gather in and re-transmit to a wider audience, fragments of the lived life.

Individually and collectively, the volumes of the Flashbacks give an account of 'what a life was' in different places. These volumes do this by giving an insight into the ways in which individuals lived their lives and how they felt about those lives. By allowing people to give their own account, in their own words, the reader gains an insight into different lives in different parts of Scotland.

This particular volume gives the recollections of a number of folk who, as children, took part in and/or observed the seasonal folk drama *Galoshins*. The role of seasonal events in the life of a child is important for a variety of reasons, one reason being that such events help the child to gain an understanding of the passage of time. Experiencing a gap between the occurrence of an event such as *Galoshins* from season to season and year to year allows the child to feel how long passage of a season and a year 'feels'. As the child ages, the interval, though the same chronologically, begins to feel shorter and so an awareness of the changing nature of the passage of time is inculcated. In a very real sense, events such as *Galoshins* help the young person and their older audience, at some level, to reflect on the fleeting nature of existence. Notwithstanding this ascription of meaning, the most important function and outcome of *Galoshins* should not be forgotten – fun. What emerges clearly in what follows is that planning, participation and performance of *Galoshins* gave to those involved great enjoyment and many happy memories.

The essence of the 'Flashbacks' series is the everyday life of as broad a sample of people as possible – even everyday life at times of seasonal celebration. Everyday life is often held to be that which is lived in between interesting events, with those events constituting our stories or our histories. However, it is in the everyday that we meet most people; that we prepare and eat meals; that we raise our children and that we engage in work and other activities. In short, it is in the everyday that we live most of our lives. The accounts given in this volume add to the Flashbacks project which will continue with further volumes by different people – perhaps even you.

Mark A. Mulhern, Editor
EUROPEAN ETHNOLOGICAL RESEARCH CENTRE
EDINBURGH 2011

GALOSHINS REMEMBERED

Introduction

The Play as a House-Visiting Custom

THE recollections in this book relate to the house-visiting *Galoshins* custom as found throughout the south of Scotland in the early part of the twentieth century and at the very end of the nineteenth. The performances remembered can sometimes be precisely dated, but some of the dates given are necessarily approximate. The recollections are organised by area: [1–5] being from the south-east; [6–10] moving to the south-west; and [10–14] being from the central belt.

'A penny was a lot in these days' was the comment of William Brown of Melrose [2], and many others echoed the idea. Mrs Hunter in Biggar, for example, said 'a halfpenny could get you quite a lot then' and added that 'if you gathered a sixpence you felt you were rich'.[3] The collecting of money was a main feature of the *Galoshins* activity. Elsie Boag observed as a little girl aged seven or eight that the boys in Gargunnock 'went all round about to the big houses and to the manse and to the farms and the next day they were boasting about what they had made'.[4] We can see that it was prestigious to have made a good haul!

The gangs of boys who typically performed the play in people's houses in the first half of the twentieth century were strongly motivated by the desire to collect the pennies that were willingly given to them at the correct season of year for the time of their performance. And the mention of the 'correct' season brings us straight to the point that it can be difficult to make all-embracing statements about any folk tradition since traditional practice is always marked by variation. The play was performed at one of two seasons: either on Old Year's Night (31 December) and in the period leading up to it, which was often about a week but could be longer; or on, or sometimes close to, Halloween (31 October). In any particular place, it was performed as a house-visiting custom only once in the year, and the boys would be expected either during the winter season that can be called Yule or at Halloween. And even this seasonal connection was not static, since a district could change from one to the other over the course of time and we can find traces of a movement from Yule to Halloween.[5] This sometimes shows up in the songs and rhymes, which may contain references to Christmas, New Year or Hogmanay, even when the performance takes place at Halloween. Jim MacQueen in Gargunnock[6] performed at Halloween and his text included the lines:

> For we're children out to play,
> Out to seek our Hogmanay.

Of course, we cannot be quite certain from an indication like this that the whole play had been transferred to the different season, but we do sometimes have definite information about a change of season as, for example, in the case of Morebattle where Harry Fox [3] performed at Halloween while his father, Tom Fox, performed at Yule.

Although the play was normally done at only one point in the year, the boys (or sometimes, more generally, the children) might go round the houses at another time also with other forms of appeal for a gift. The times like this that are still remembered are identical or similar to those in which the play was performed – Halloween and a day in the vicinity of the New Year, sometimes Hansel Monday (the first Monday in the year). These visits belonged to the total pattern of collecting from the inhabitants and wishing well to the community of which *Galoshins* formed a part, and several accounts of customs like this and the associated rhymes are included in this book. The appeal I remember vividly myself was when I was in Crail on the coast of Fife in 1950 and two little girls came to the door on the last day of the year and said together:

> Oor feet's cauld, oor shin's thin,
> Gie's oor Hogmanay and let's rin.

Money is seldom mentioned in connection with the other house-visiting customs besides the play, and the gifts seem to have consisted mainly of foods of various kinds.

At an earlier period in history, there was also some collecting at other times of year. Eggs were gathered by children going round the houses at Easter and there was also a collection for a sport that is now illegal – cock-fighting.[7] We should remember the existence of this custom in connection with the *Galoshins* play for here again we have two opponents that fight until one is killed or vanquished. In this case, though, there is no resurrection of the slain combatant. Boys used to go round farmhouses begging for cocks that they could enter into the fights. The boys were identified with their birds and the owner of the victorious cock was given the name of king. Clearly the idea of a ritual conflict at a set time of year is not confined to the opponents in *Galoshins*. Neill Martin has pointed to connections with the ball games still played in Kirkwall and also in Jedburgh and other Borders towns and villages, and a tug-of-war that used to take place in Stromness, and has argued that the reconciliation that follows the conflict is more important than the conflict itself.[8] Even in the case of the cock-fighting that was lethal to many of the birds, the contest ended with a feast for all the boys involved. In *Galoshins*, the combatants and other actors come together at the close in a brotherly way which is emphasised by their singing together; and they all call down blessings on their hosts so that everyone present is brought into a communion where gifts and good wishes are exchanged. The boys then go on to the next house, so creating a chain of goodwill through the whole village or other bounded area.

The boys had a definite territory, but how it was defined varied according to circumstances. In some places it was accepted that the householders would receive and pay out to more than one gang and there the competition was less intense than in places where only one performance was rewarded. Even where more than one gang was allowed to perform, there was an expectation that those who got there first would get a better welcome. The boys went where they were confident that they had the right to go, and the area might be a street or a section of a village or even the country area round a village as far as it was feasible to walk in an evening.

When the custom weakened in strength, there was a tendency to cover only the immediate area and to go less far. Whatever area was covered, there was a frisson of excitement in the challenge that other gangs of boys were out on the same errand. It could be simply a matter of a mix of gangs of boys who might come to cat-calling or threatened blows when they came up against each other, or the operation might be subject to tight definitions so that specific areas belonged to one or other gang and to knowingly 'work' the territory of another was an open challenge. There were taboos, and breaking them was clearly an additional excitement to some, while others were content to abide within their own restricted area.

The following precise account of territorial divisions in and around the village of Kippen came from William Hay, who was just too young to take part before the custom ceased there during World War I. In his experience, the play was normally confined to the one night, Hogmanay.

WH You see there were more than one lot of boys went round the village. There were maybe three or four lots, and they may have once sleeked out the night before and did a turn of the village, some of the houses anyway.

EL Would you just go round the village?

WH Yes, just round the village. They each had their districts where they done well, they always tried to get there first, you know. Sometimes there was a bit of poaching on the districts, you know, but mostly they agreed on the districts they were doing. One done the Fore Road, the other would do the Station Road and a part of the village, and one would do the Burnside. And another lot would maybe do Cauldhame up here at that time.

EL And how would they decide who was doing which?

WH Well, they talked it over at the school, usually.

EL And you all went out usually at the same time?

WH Yes, but they didn't always stick to their bargains, sometimes they were broken. …

EL Which district did [your brother] go out to? Different ones, I suppose?

WH Well, he done – in the squad he was in, he did the Fore Road, that was down to Arngomery, the big house down there; that was usually their last call on that road.[9]

The guisers performing the play nearly always set out after dark, but there was occasionally some daytime activity.[10] Jock Simpson of Gargunnock, remembering *Galoshins* at Halloween, spoke of starting out at nine in the morning and going round about six farms during the day and then performing in the village at night; he recognised that he must have been remembering a Saturday since he would have had to be at school during the week.[11] The norm, of course, was to perform in people's houses, but again there could be exceptions.[12] W. Knox, writing about the play in a letter of March 1982, said: 'This was performed in Hawick about 60 years ago. I remember seeing it done in a back green at Laing Terrace.'

The boys usually either blackened their faces or wore papier mâché 'false faces', although some guisers refrained from doing more than applying beards and moustaches so as not to present a frightening appearance that could scare young children. The face-blackening was not total. As William Hay described it, 'it was jist a smear here on the cheeks and across the forehead and maybe a little on the nose and round the ear'.[13] Mr Hay also mentioned blackening along the back of the hands and fingers. The blackening was normally done with soot, as in this case, or with burnt cork, but there was a memory of guisers in Morebattle having their faces smeared with a mixture of soot and oil by the blacksmith.[14] There is sometimes mention of disguise being so complete there was difficulty in recognising the boys, although their voices were not normally disguised and often allowed them to be identified. Elsie Boag commented: 'There must have been five or six of them come in, in a crowd you know, and they were all dressed up. We didn't know them at all until they spoke. One or two of them we recognised the voices, but they were so well disguised that you wouldn't be able to tell who they were.'[15] Miss Boag spoke of both face-blackening and the wearing of false faces and, in this case, the boys may have had on false faces which obscured their faces completely.

Walter Culbertson, who had sold masks in his village shop in Morebattle, remembered the transition to wearing them during the play.

WC What we used to call false faces ... they were sorta shaped like the face and you put it over your face and made yourself look awful. ... And you'd a bit of elastic or a piece of string, but usually a bit of elastic or an elastic band from the holes round the back of the head. ... Over Christmas time they used to go what they called guising and they wore them then. They used to go from house to house, maybe three or four, and give the householder a little concert. ... Sometimes they acted a little play and they very often wore the masks then. ...

EL Do you remember them blackening their faces as well sometimes?

WC	Sometimes, before masks ... but that went off when the masks had to come.
EL	And did you actually sell the masks? ...
WC	Yes, a penny each, one penny. ... That was in the 1920s. ... We bought them once a year ... at the end o the summer. A traveller would come round and sell them, and we bought in enough to do all the winter. Sometimes you were sold out or sometimes you had maybe a dozen left. ...
EL	You probably did the play yourself, of course, when you were young, did you? And did you blacken your face?
WC	Yes, yes. It wasn't masks when I was a boy, you'd just blacken your face, just rub in the soot.[16]

Mr Culbertson commented later that, even when masks came into use, some boys could not afford them and so would simply blacken their faces.[17]

The boys performing the play in the early twentieth century had generally learned it orally from slightly older boys. There were no widely circulated fixed texts in use in this period, so far as the evidence goes, and I came across no mention of learning from print, even though play texts had been published in books and newspapers. Play texts had also been included in chapbooks (small booklets): these were used as sources on occasion at an earlier period when chapbooks were circulating more widely than they were in the twentieth century and when the play texts used in performance were longer and so a little more difficult to master.[18] Of course, any texts originally learned from chapbooks could have remained in traditional use, and the chapbook texts themselves could have been taken from oral performances so that no hard-and-fast lines can be drawn. St George played a prominent part in some chapbooks and had lines like those used in the text known to Mrs M. Williamson, aged 75, who wrote from Norfolk in response to the *Scots Magazine* appeal of January 1982. She recalled that she, as 'the littlest one', was only allowed to sing a song in a performance in which her brother played Doctor Brown when they went out guising at Halloween in Threemiletown near Linlithgow. The play included the words:

> I am St George, the noble champion bold,
> And with my broad sword I won £10,000s worth of gold.
> 'Twas I who fought the fiery dragon and brought him to the slaughter,
> And by that means, I won the King of Egypt's daughter.

I quoted this in a follow-up letter to *The Scots Magazine* in April 1982 and William Walker wrote in with other St George lines that came from the play as performed by his father in the Springburn Road and Petershill area of Glasgow:

> I remember my Father who was born in 1875 reciting with suitable gestures, words of the Guiser Play, the *Goloshans*.
>
> > I am St George, the Champion Bold
> > And with my claymore win pots of gold.
> > I fight fiery dragons to their knees
>
> The final words I am afraid have been forgotten but they did not refer to the King of Egypt's daughter.

Mrs Sheila Duffy's version [7] is the only one given here to include St George, and it has other similarities to the chapbook form of the play.[19] A further mention of St George comes from Elizabeth M. C. Sanderson of Edinburgh (letter of 12.5.1982), whose account includes an interesting reference to the costume worn by the boys who performed at Hogmanay in Galashiels:

> My father used to tell me about how he played Galatian in Galashiels, Selkirkshire, when he was a young boy. That would be in the 1870s as he was born in 1864. ... He definitely called the chief character Galatian, not Goloshan or Goshan, and he

fought St George. ... All the players blacked their faces and wore their white shirts loose over their trousers.

I was very struck by the way that many people who remembered the play had sharp images of it, and my questions were often intended just to keep them telling the rest of us what it was that they could 'see' so vividly with the mind's eye. The costumes and setting, for example, were often remembered in great detail and this allows us to invoke total pictures as well as to follow the words and action of the play.

The Action of the Play

The play can be seen as falling into the following parts, each one associated with a particular character or characters: the entry and the prologue (MC, master of ceremonies), the challenge and the fight (two champions), the cure (doctor), the blessing (all), the appeal (treasurer). This takes five boys, but often there was no MC, and four could do the play quite adequately. The boys could even manage with three at a pinch, leaving out the treasurer.

THE ENTRY AND THE PROLOGUE

The entry had its own excitement. The boys were coming in from the outside into a home and practice varied. Sometimes they simply entered, with or without knocking beforehand, but more often they asked for permission with some such words as, 'Will you let the guisers act?' At any rate, this was the point of first engagement with the household, and, if they were unwelcome, there might be friction. The first words spoken are sometimes taken as the name of the character who speaks them so that we have actors who said they took the parts of 'Stir Up' or 'Keep Silence'. Both these characters are giving instructions to the audience: one telling them to 'stir up the fire' to give light for the performance and the other telling them to keep quiet. In one case [7], a character called Bessie sweeps the floor with a broom beforehand.[20] The boy in the role of MC may introduce himself, as in 'In comes Little I' [3], and speak a prologue, and he may later call other characters onto the 'stage'. Andrew Rennie of Kippen [14], who played this part, referred to him as the head man or the boss and William Hay from the same village, but from a later period called him the head lad. Mr Hay described his costume as he knew it:

WH   He'd a sorta tweed suit, we would say, long trousers, jacket, collar and tie. And he'd this sort of soft Donegal hat, and his walking stick.
EL   Yes, quite a picture. Did he use the stick, then?
WH   Oh, he jist carried it under his arm like that, like an officer in the army, under his arm.[21]

James Anderson [11], in the account he published of the play, describes the presenter he saw, called the Talking Man, as another kind of authority figure. He 'had a likeness to the Master of Ceremonies of a circus'. In his follow-up letter to Paul Smith, Mr Anderson said: 'The Talking Man had a cut away coat and was the best dressed of the lot, something like a ringmaster at a circus. He carried a dog whip.'

THE CHALLENGE AND THE FIGHT

The action here requires a challenger, who often expects 'to win the game', and a warrior who takes up the challenge and is often best identified by his opening words 'The game sir', as indicated in the table on page 24. At the end of the fighting one of the combatants is killed. This is the challenger in nearly all the cases of a single death included here, but it is sometimes his opponent who dies, as in the versions from William Brown [2] and from Jim MacQueen in Gargunnock.[22] In the version from David

Kerr [10], both of the combatants and all their supporters are killed.[23] The Doctor usually addresses the slain man by a different name and the name he uses is included in brackets in the table. As with many other features of the play, there is variation, but we can say firmly that there is a fight which results in the death of one or more of the combatants. The name 'Galoshins', which is given to one of the combatants as well as to the custom, has been something of a puzzle. Hayward suggests that it was derived from the footwear worn by the guisers and does actually have a distant connection with the word 'galoshes', meaning overshoes, just as one might guess from the similarity in sound.[24]

THE CURE

The character who has done the killing often then expresses regret, sometimes saying that he has killed a brother, son or cousin of his, and the Doctor, who is almost always called Doctor Brown, is called in. It will take an exceptional degree of skill to bring a dead man back to life, and clearly the doctor who achieves this must be assumed to have magical powers. The audience is invited into a fairytale world, rather like pantomime perhaps, where it accepts that things can happen outside normal experience. Already, of course, the fight of the champions has been remote from everyday life. There is nothing solemn, or even serious, about the exercise of the Doctor's abilities; he is always a source of laughter. At the same time, it is worth noting that a part of the audience often consisted of small children and that, for at least one young boy, the death was experienced as real and so the Doctor's cure was also felt to be real. James H. Leishman, writing from Wick, said: 'I could not have been more than 5 or 6 yrs of age, at the time (1918?) when 'the "guisers" were welcomed in, to our home, at Thornton, Fife. ... [T]he sword play had a traumatic effect, to say the least, and the "body" gave great cause for concern. What relief then when the Dr.'s attentions proved successful!'

	CHALLENGER	**RESPONDENT**
1. Purves	Galoshins (John)	unnamed 'The game sir'
2. Brown	Galashans	Jack 'The game sir' (Jack)
3. Fox	Galashin	The Game Sir 'The game sir'
4. Crosby	Galoshins (young man)	Horatio 'The game sir'
5. Ramage	Galoshins	unnamed 'The game sir'
6. Thomson	King George (Jack)	Sir William Wallace
7. Duffy	Gloshins (Jack)	St George 'The game sir'
8. Laurie (K)	Bal-Hector (Jack)	Black Knight 'The game sir'
9. Laurie (NS)	Galatians	Black Knight
10. Kerr	Sir William Wallace	Sir John Monteith
11. Anderson	Sir William Wallace (Sir William)	Robert the Bruce
12. Hendry	Galoshins	unnamed 'The game sir'
13. Wands	Jock Slasher (old man)	Goshin 'The game sir'
14. Rennie	Galoshins (old Jack)	Admiral 'The game sir'

The Doctor may simply come in and with a couple of lines of verse and a simple action (usually involving real or imagined liquid) effect the cure, but this section of the play could be spun out for some time, especially if the gang of boys included a comic who could throw himself into mime as well as the uttering of nonsense. The doctor may list all the odd-sounding ailments he can cure, or he may speak of his travels. One version [2] includes a bargaining about the doctor's fee. There is a great deal of variation among the different versions in the doctor's speeches, which are usually in prose. The longest version noted in recent times was communicated in response to the *Scots Magazine* coverage by a 13-year-old girl, Aileen Orr, writing from Edinburgh. She explained that she had heard her father who came from Douglas in Lanarkshire saying this piece and had liked it so much that she had learned it herself. This is all she knew of the play and it seems very likely that her father had enacted the role of Doctor Brown.

Doctor Brown	Here comes I old Doctor Brown,
	The best old doctor in the town.
Anon	Well doctor what can you cure?
Doctor Brown	I can cure the plague, within, without,
	Also the palsy and the gout,
	Bring me an old woman, three score and ten
	The knuckle joint of a big toe broke,
	I'll take it off and put it on again.
Anon	Well done doctor. What is your medicine?
Doctor Brown	A wee bottle in my waistcoat pocket called:
	Hens pens, peezy weezy,
	Bumbie's bacon, donkey's treacle,
	Sap of the poker, juice of the tongs,
	Three turkey's eggs, nine miles long.
	Put that in a mouse's blather,
	Stir it up with a wild pig's feather.
	Put three drops in Jack's ear

	And he'll get up and sing a song!
Jack	Once I was dead but now I'm alive,
	God bless the old doctor who made me survive.

THE COLLECTION

The character who took the collection at the end was often called Wee Johnny Funny or something similar, although Little Devil Doubt was also in evidence in versions known to Mrs Duffy [7] and Jim MacQueen.[25] This boy was often younger than the others and his youth was expected to be appealing and to bring out the generous instincts of the audience. The collector's speech hammered home his message by repeatedly mentioning money or specific coins or amounts like a sixpence, tuppence, a penny, a bawbie or, in one case, a curdie.[26]

Re-creation from Men's Memories

The play had practically died out as a boys' house-visiting custom well before the middle of the twentieth century, but sometimes men who remembered doing it were so enthusiastic that they managed to transmit the play to children and bring about a revival. Harry Fox [3], David Kerr [10] and Robert Hendry [12] were all taught by their fathers and were all acting in isolated pockets in communities where the play was no longer active outside their own troupes, although of course the tradition of Halloween guising gave them an appropriate context in which to perform.

Men must often have told their children and grandchildren about their experience of performing the play. John MacFadyen, for example, was able to give the following vivid account relating to Scotch Row in Craigneuk that came to him from his father[27]:

In regard to the *Galoshins*, he said that they went around and this was the opening. They would knock on a door and, if they were allowed in, the first one in would start off by saying:

> A room, a room, brave gallant boys.
> Stir up the fire and give us light
> For in this room there'll be a fight.

And I could understand; they might've had gas in Scotch Row, but it might've been paraffin lamps, so that there was some point in stirring up the fire to give them light. And according to him the fight, the contest that took place, was between Bruce and De Boone and then he mentioned Doctor Brown, and then at the end, he had this part as Wee Johnnie Funny. ... And one of the instances that stuck in my mind was that after one of their performances in one of the houses, in the corner of the room, or the corner of the kitchen, actually, there was the bine or the tub that they'd used to wash themselves when they'd come in from their work. And it was still there, still full of dirty water, and when they finished their performance the young sons of the house, I presume, grabbed up the bine, the tub. They saw what was coming, they rushed for the door, got stuck in the entry and got the whole bine thrown over them as their reward for their performance!

Sometimes adults who remembered the play would perform it for a child audience. James Hunter in Dunfermline used to act out *Galatians* every Hogmanay for five or six years in the late 1930s and early 1940s for his grandson, Ian Hunter, from whom I recorded the following account in Edinburgh.[28]

My grandfather was born in 1864 ... and when he was in his seventies he used to tell me about how he went guising and this was always on Hogmanay, ... and on Hogmanay he used to act out the play of *Galatians*. He acted all the parts himself. And I was absolutely enthralled by this and a bit intimidated by it too because it was all very dramatic. And I used to ask him to tell me more about it and to do it again. ... This would be guising in the village of Kingseat, which was a coal-mining village, ... in the 1870s. ... On the evening of Hogmanay [a group of youngsters] would go out and start visiting some of the neighbouring houses who were expecting them. And the play started with one of the characters standing forward and he declaims:

> Here come I, Galatians,
> Galatians is my name.
> Sword and pistol by my side
> I hope to win the game.

And then another character stands forward and says:

> The game sir, the game sir,
> It isna in your power.
> Now I draw my trusty sword
> And fell you to the floor.

And they proceed to have a sword fight. And in the process of this Galatians is killed. And the other character is aghast at this.

> What have I done?
> I've slain my very brother.
> What shall I do?
> I'll never have another.

And then either he or some of the other characters hit on a plan.

> Send for Doctor Brown
> The best doctor in the town.

And Doctor Brown steps forward.

> Here come I, Doctor Brown,
> The best doctor in the town.

And he holds up his bottle of medicine which is called inky pinky and talks about – I don't remember the details there – but he talks about the ills that it can cure, and the only thing I can remember is the rout and the gout. And then he starts to work on Galatians and he says:

> Some on your nose, some on your bum,
> Gie inky pinky time to work, up ye come.

And Galatians leaps up and everybody rejoices. Galatians says:

> Once I was dead, now I revive,
> Blessd be the doctor that brought me alive.

And the other character embraces him and he says:

> Let's join hands and be freends thegither,
> We'll never fight again but help one anither.

And then all the characters join hands and they sometimes do a dance. And then they turn round and they address the audience and they say:

> Blessd be the maister of this hoose, blessd be the mistress tae,
> Blessd be all the bairnies that in this hoose will grow.
> Lang may your lum reek, may you never shed a tear,
> We wish you many a Hogmanay and good New Year.

And that's the end of the play and then after the applause they get eatables – oranges or apples or cakes and sometimes ginger wine – and then they take themselves off and they go to the next house.

Obviously for him the acting of it was essential and I mean I can remember actually being quite frightened on some occasions because he had a poker for a sword and his shadow was up on the wall behind him and I really thought, you know, he was going to demolish the house! He was acting – he couldn't *not* act it – that was an intrinsic part of the whole thing.

Men who had enjoyed the play as boys conceived the idea of performing the play as a monologue to an adult audience. Andrew Rennie [14] had kept the play alive for the community in Kippen by performing a monologue on pensioners' evenings, so it was not too strange to him to put on an extra performance for a video recording. James Wands [13] mentioned in his correspondence: 'I have played this as a one man; just like Tommy Cooper for a laugh; I used different hats and a bonnet.' When I was recording Mr Wands in March 1982 it turned out that he was still doing this and that his most recent performance had been in the previous year[29]:

EL   And then you did it sometimes on your own, did you, a one-man show?

JW   Oh aye, I've did it doon at the bowling club, the veterans' night, jist wi different hats, jist for a laugh.

EL   Just quite recently, was this?

JW   Well, well, last year I did it.

EL   Oh you did! Well, no wonder it was fresh in your mind! Have you got the hats still that you made then?

JW   No, they were doon in the club.

EL   But you used the same old style with feathers, did you?

JW   Ugh well, sometimes when ye couldnae get a feather, ye jist put a bit soft paper or something on it, stuck it on a hat. Stir Up Yer Fire does the whole and then when he's finished wi that, 'Here comes in Jock Slasher', ye just take that hat off and go on, move aboot, ye ken, and then just come in wi that hat on. When one speaks, you change the hats, you know. Have you never seen Tommy Cooper at it, eh? Tommy

Cooper did, no this thing but something – And then when Doctor Brown comes in you've a saft, usually a soft hat on for Doctor Brown come in. And of course when he's finished speaking, Jock Slasher gets into his hat, and this is hoo ye carry on. And this is whaur the laugh comes in, ye sometimes pit [on] the wrong hat, then ye go back and get the right hat! ... And yer wee widden sword! Och aye!

Sometimes, too, a man took part with a child or children in a home production of the play. Mrs Senga Trotter, Bo'ness, had acted in the play with her grandfather, who was originally from Linlithgow and had lived most of his life in Bo'ness. She wrote about it with evident excitement in a letter published in *The Scots Magazine* in March 1982:

[On finding David Fergus's article 'Here Comes in Goloshans'] I could hardly believe what I was reading – outside my own family, I had never come across anyone who had ever heard of Goloshans!

As a small child in the early 1940s, I remember very well taking part in this little play. My grandfather, William Nimmo, had introduced my brother, sister and myself to Goloshans. By the time I was five, my brother and sister were in their mid-teens and much too grown-up to take part in the play, so I played most of the parts, a feat achieved by stepping right to left and removing a hat, helped out by Grandfather, then in his seventies.

Our play was a scaled down version of that related by David Fergus. It was usually performed at Hallowe'en and on New Year's Day and always preceded the 'party pieces' or, as Grandfather put it, 'The Guisartin.' Props were very simple, a hat, shawl, gloves and the porridge spurtle for a weapon.

The proceedings began with Brave Alexander appearing to tell the assembled company of the entertainment in store. Goloshans would then strut in, saying, 'Here comes in Goloshans, Goloshans is my name, sword and pistol by my side, I'm out to win the game!'

In the fight with Brave Alexander that ensued, Goloshans would fall to the ground, mortally wounded, calling out, 'Send for good old Dr Brown, the best old doctor in the town.' Doctor Brown would come with his bottle of Inky Pinky which, he claimed, could cure the gout, the colic, the scurvy, the ring worm and the root-mi-scoot! Once the potion had been applied to nose and toes, the Doctor would declare, 'Up Jack, and sing a song!' Then Jack (the slain Goloshans) would spring up and intone, 'Once I was dead, but now I'm alive, thanks to good old Doctor Brown, I am alive.' Only then, after the Goloshans saga, could the family do their 'turns'.

Rather amazingly, in the case of the Crosby family [4] the play was passed down within the home like this over two generations and performed into the 1990s.

Women's Memories and Girl Performers

Women as well as men had vivid memories of the play that had once been performed round the houses. Isobel Robb in Newtown St Boswells, for example, published a version remembered by her mother in 1966,[30] and she remembered it herself, too, and was later able to give me the tune of the closing song[31]:

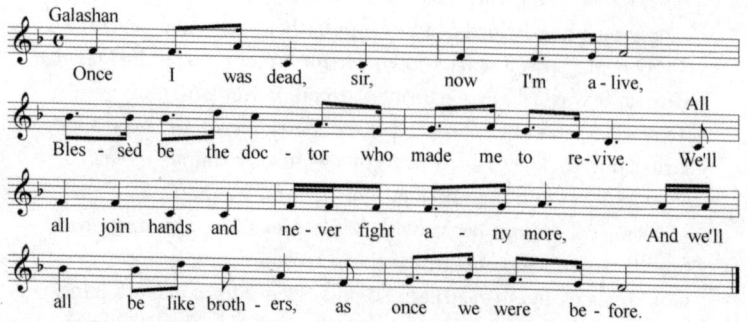

[NB: Please note that the music in this book has not been transcribed at pitch.]

Girls occasionally took part in the play, something that probably became more common when the boys' interest in the tradition slackened. Mrs Margaret Cockburn (letter of 10.3.82), said she had performed in the play as a child in Innerleithen 'as part of our guising repertoire' around 1937–38, having been taught the words by her mother who remembered seeing the play performed by boys in Hawick in the early 1900s.

However, the play was not a male preserve entirely even at an earlier stage. We have a record that three girls gave Halloween performances of the play, as learned from other children, in the period between 1899 and 1909 in Tillicoultry, Clackmannanshire. They were Agnes Hardie (later Mrs Smith) and her sister Annie and a friend, Mary Hunter, who took the roles respectively of the King of Macedonia, Galashin and the Doctor and 'went up and down the streets knocking on the doors, asking if they wanted guisers'.[32] Mrs Smith taught the play to her three children – two sons and a daughter – who performed it at Halloween, the girl, Anne, always playing the part of the Doctor. They performed first in Darnley, near Glasgow, and then, in neighbours' houses, in Nottingham. The play, as written out by Anne (Mrs Pratt letter, 18.11.1980), has two unusual features in the latter part which is given here: first, an unmasking precedes the announcement that it is a close relative of the challenger who has been killed, and, second, the part of the song when 'the three join hands and walk round in a circle' includes a repeat.

> The fight takes place. Galatia [pronounced 'Galashee'] drops to the floor. The king bends over him, removes his mask, and says:
> *King of Macedonia*
>> Horrible, horrible what have I done?
>> Ruined myself and killed my son.
>> Is there not a doctor in the town who can cure this man?
> *Doctor Brown*
>> Sir I am Dr Brown.
>> The finest doctor in the town.

I have a little inky pinky in my waistcoat pocket.
Put a little to his nose
And a little to his toes.
Rise up now and sing a song.

Galatia: Once I was dead and now I'm alive
Blessèd be the doctor who made me revive.
All: And we'll all join hands and we'll fight no more
And we'll all be friends as we were before.
Yes, we'll all join hands and we'll fight no more
And we'll all be friends as we were before.

Wat Ramage [5] was accustomed to girls being involved in the performance, but it is clear from his accounts that boys took the acting roles. Similarly, Mrs Mollie Strang (*née* Simpson), aged 80 when recorded, remembered taking part in the play, but evidently only as one of the bystanders. She had a vivid little girl's memory of an exciting evening[33]:

> When I would be about seven or eight year old, I stayed at an estate called Touch about three or four miles from Stirling and when Halloween came round my brothers and people next door – one or two girls there – we used to go out guising at Halloween and of course we were all dressed up. We had all false faces, I do remember, and possibly a turnip lantern, and I know myself that I had my father's slipper on ma head for a hat and going from house to house I think I carried it oftener in my hand

than it would be on ma head, it was always slipping off. And we knocked at the door and asked to come in and we did our little party piece, ye see, which was 'Here come I Galoshin, Galoshin is my name. ...' I only remember the one time doing it ... this lovely moonlight night. ... It were just a lovely night for going out, and I can always remember the owls because we were a wee bit frightened before our brothers told us it was owls that was screeching.

Fragments of a Disappearing Play

Mrs Strang was eventually able to recall all the text of the play when she was talking it over, but a few lines of the Doctor's had stayed with her all along, and she had passed them on to her daughters as part of guising tradition. She commented: 'I may have said to them we used to do this Doctor Brown. I would only start at the Doctor Brown because that was all I would remember.' Her daughter Isobel (Mrs Jenkins) said:

> The only bit I remember was the bit about taking out the bottle and it was:
>
> > Put a little to his nose
> > And a little to his toes.
> > Rise up, Jack, and sing.
>
> That's the only bit I can remember and I mean it must really have been mother that, when we would be going out guising, she would give us a little bottle with water in it and we had to say this. Why, I don't know, because we didn't know the rest of the play.[34]

Very little of the play survives in this scrap offered by Isobel and her sister Ina as part of their Halloween guising. A slightly longer, but still truncated, form was known to William Bruce, Newtown St Boswells. He had an interesting memory from the early 1920s of guising done by a group of boys – and one girl who 'used to play football in the park wi us a lot, she always went out along wi the boys, a bit of a tomboy'. He recalled[35]:

> On Halloween night we'd get four or five of us together. We'd really go to each other's houses but, if we thought there was a chance of getting an extra copper or two, we would go to other houses, you know, and probably get an apple and an orange and well we – jist the favourite one was, two of us would have wooden swords, jist, and a toy pistol and we'd ask, when we came to the door, say: 'Have you anything for the guisers?' or 'Could we come in and act?' … And then the one would challenge the other wi the swords, you know, and the favourite one was:
>
>> Here come in Galashin,
>> Galashin is my name.
>> Sword and pistol by my side
>> I hope to win the game.
>
> And the other would say:
>
>> The game sir. You sir. I sir.
>> Take your sword and try sir.
>
> And then one o them always fell down and the other stood sword up and his foot on his chest, the victor. And then probably some of the rest o them would sing a song, you know, and then we would get the copper or whatever they gave us, and we'd go to another house.

I checked with Mr Bruce, and the second speaker definitely said as one speech the words that are normally split between the two combatants. It was clear from further discussion that the one who fell down was thought to be dead but there was no development to a revival.

So we find a death without any following action and, in the previous case, a cure without any preceding death. These minimal presentations seem to take the play past the limits of what can be reckoned a coherent performance. But up to this point of disintegration, there was much to be said for brevity.

The Players and the Community

It could, in fact, be argued that, as an art form in a community setting, *Galoshins* had achieved a perfect balance. The short play was fairly fixed and required thought and preparation and a group spirit to be successful. The text, although sometimes a bit odd, was always vigorous, and it allowed for some improvisation. The pairing of the play with free-choice rhymes, songs and music gave extra scope to the talented. The small number of characters worked well in the limited space of people's homes. And the swift movement from house to house spread youthful exuberance throughout the whole community and enabled the boys to gather the maximum number of pennies in the limited time at their disposal.

GALOSHINS

Recollections from the Players and Observers

1 *James Purves – Melrose, 1897–1899*

I recorded James W. Purves in the back of the family antique shop in Melrose on 25 August 1977 (SA1977.205B) and he told me then that he lived at Sundean, Douglas Road, Melrose and that he would be 92 on his next birthday on 7 January 1978. Since his date of birth was 1885, and since he told me the boys that performed were aged about twelve to fourteen, the performances he remembered can be placed right at the end of the nineteenth century.

EL   I'd be very interested in anything about the New Year, what you did at Hogmanay.

JP   Hogmanay. Oh well, Hogmanay was just the usual procedure, every New Year you went round the houses. … And the great act was Galashin, Galoshin, Galashin, he was the man. Who Galashin was I don't know. He must've been a warrior or someone who just travelled about throwing about his weight, I suppose, because it starts off, the boy that comes in as Galashin:

> Here comes in Galashin,
> Galashin is my name,
> Wi sword an pistol by my side
> I hope to win the game.

Then another boy comes in, You, sir?
He says, I, sir.
Take your sword and try, sir.

And then they both pull out swords and start fighting. Imaginary stuff. And one gets knocked down, you see. Then from the side comes Doctor Brown.

> Here comes in old Doctor Brown,
> The best old doctor in the town.

And he pulls out a bottle, and:

> Put a little to his head and a little to his toes,
> Rise up John and sing a song.

So this boy immediately gets up, he's cured, and he sings that song:

> Once I was dead and now I'm alive,
> And blessed be the doctor that made me to revive.

And, well, that's the end of it.
EL Do you remember the tune at all?
JP The tune, oh yes, well let's think. Yes. I remember the tune. That Doctor Brown bit?
EL Yes.

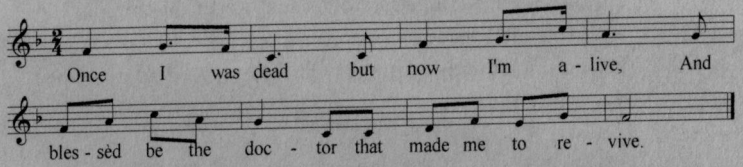

JP It's just two lines, but that's the tune.

EL Yes, great! And then you got given things by the people, did you, after that, in the house?

JP Well, there'd be odd songs sung by any of the boys. One would sing a song, just oh any old song, any Scots song, and then that would be the finish. It only lasted for about seven minutes or so, the whole scene, that was the end of it.

EL How many of you would there be?

JP Oh the average would be four, sometimes three. But the average turnout for a thing like that would be four.

EL What would the fourth one do? Because there were two of them fighting and then there'd be the doctor –

JP There's the two fighting, Galashin and this other boy that took him on, yes, that's right. Aye, that was the average, four. But they were always glad to get the thing over and get outside, you know they'd no patience inside. It was trying for them. It was all unrehearsed really. It'd be gone over somewhere once, that's all. It wasn't a thing you'd rehearsed for a few days and improved upon it or anything like that. It was all just handed down from father to son and these boys next year might be doing the very same thing. Same tune, same songs, same people.

EL And you took one of these parts, did you?

JP Yes, yes.

EL Do you remember what you were?

JP I can't remember. I wasn't any of the main ones anyway. I used to sing a song I think, but I can't remember the name of the song. You were supposed to do something, each one, but they were all fidgeting to get out, to get the thing over with and get outside.

EL It would start with a little play and then you'd all do something after that?

JP Yes.

EL Where did you go? Which houses did you visit?

JP Well they were out the Weir Hill there, out High Cross Avenue, these big houses there. And eh, well they all had

	plenty of money and at that time of year they were quite willing and ready to ask boys in. And if they had a young family, well they were watching the thing too.
EL	And I think you said they sometimes knew you, did they? The people in the houses recognised you?
JP	Some would recognise, of course. You were guisers, they called them. You were supposed to be disguised but they had to find out who you were, definitely.
EL	What sort of things did you wear?
JP	Oh, your face blackened and eh, something over your eyes. Not very much. A funny hat on. Anything like that.
EL	Would the doctor wear something special?
JP	The Doctor was just, I think he'd just a black coat. That's all he had, aye.
EL	And what about the fellows fighting, they had swords had they, the lads that were fighting?
JP	Well, they were more like, I don't know, more like warriors, you know. And they tried to get real swords, I remember, they weren't dummies.
EL	Really!
JP	No, they had things aboot that length, real swords.
EL	Real metal ones?
JP	Metal, yes.
EL	It must've been realistic.
JP	You know there was never any accidents happened with them as far as I can remember.
EL	If they had proper swords, did they dress up like soldiers or anything like that?
JP	Well, they were supposed to be in some sort of uniform of some kind, you know. They were supposed to be fighting men, soldiers or something, but nothing that we knew anything about. They disguised themselves – that's where it got its name, guisers. The people that you went to weren't supposed to know who you were.
EL	Did anyone collect with a hat?

JP   No, no, they didn't go round with a hat or anything, but they collected things, stuff to eat, wee cakes and things like that, and put them in bags. Each one got something. And then sometimes you might get tuppence each on an average, for yer performance.

EL   And I think you said you might go out two nights in the year, did you?

JP   It's quite possible that we went out two nights.

EL   Which nights would that be?

JP   Oh I don't know. It depends on the – you see, if it happened in the end of a week it's quite possible we'd go out on a Friday night and also on the Saturday night, but the Sunday was taboo. There were no Sunday performances.

EL   Was this the night of Hogmanay then, and the night just before it?

JP   That's right.

EL   You've got a very good memory of it.

JP   Oh, it's a thing of the past. You're reviving my memory because I'd clean forgotten about the whole thing.

EL   Really! Did you enjoy doing it?

JP   Oh yes, we liked doing it. Just something out of the ordinary.

EL   Do you remember at all the people that you did it with? Was it the same group that did it year after year?

JP   We didn't go to too many; on an average night going out I suppose we would be, five or six would be the limit, sometimes only four. But sometimes they made an awful fuss of you, you know. They would get things all arranged in their dining room or wherever you were and they would get seats all round like for an audience and a sort of imitation stage that you performed on, and there had to be a door, an exit in and out, oh yes.

EL   You'd get nervous when all that was happening.

JP   Well it made one nervous seeing all these people because all their friends and relatives that were there staying with them at that time, they brought them all in to witness this

	Galashin. But I think most of them were greatly disappointed because it was nothing really.
EL	Was it always boys only, that did it?
JP	No, there were no women, no girls, no.
EL	Were any of the boys dressed up as girls?
JP	No, they were all boys. I've never known of any girls doing it, it was jist a boys' thing. ...
EL	What age d'you think you'd have been when you saw it being done? I mean, sorry, when you did it yourself, what sort of age were you?
JP	Oh well, the average age of the people that were in – well now, let's think. There was a very prominent boy, Hart, when I was a boy, William Hart. Now he was an apprentice in a bank doon the High Street and he'd just joined up and one of the people that we were going to perform was the head banker that employed him, you see. And he would be, his age would be then about, now let me think, just after he left school about twelve, thirteen or fourteen, round about there. That's about the average age for them at that time.

2 William Brown – Melrose, 1912–1913

I paid my first visit to William (Doc) Brown in Darnick, Melrose, on 27 August 1977 (SA1977.205B3), two days after I visited Mr Purves, and recorded him again on 8 October 1979 (SA1979.091.B1). Mr Brown belonged to the next generation and recalled the play as it was performed in Melrose just before World War I. He worked as a chauffeur for a time and was later a mechanic both in civilian life and in the RAF during World War II. In 2003 I asked his son, William B. Brown, in Melrose, if he had ever heard his father talking about the play and he had this to say:

Yes, he used to quote often aboot that – if we was having a big meal or something – he used to quote that bit aboot 'the mountains o beef and the rivers o gravy'; he used to quote that. Nobody ever called him – well, my mother's relations called him Bill – but everybody else locally he was always Doc Brown. And even when he was a boy, I believe, he went on the baker's van and some woman was getting her bakeries one day and she says to this – he was a character, this Tom Lillicoe that drove the van and dad was his vanboy – and the woman asked who this lad was, you see, and, 'Oh,' he says, 'this is Doctor Brown, the finest doctor in the town. He cured a woman with a boil on her arm as big as a church steeple and got it down to a pinhead all in one day.' And he used to quote that about Tom Lillicoe and he was the baker's vanman. Dad done the running up the closes and things like that, I think. (SA2003.060)

Since he got his nickname, Doc, from the play, both he and his friends had a constant reminder of it and, when I made enquiries in Melrose, I was immediately directed to him by Mrs Nairn who introduced me and was present at the first recording. The conversation below is from the 1979 recording. The play text is the second version given then, which has been inserted at the point where the text was first spoken; the account of the fight is from the first version. In the 1977 recording, Mr Brown described the duel as 'a clatter with two pokers' and the bargaining started from £50 and went to £20 and then £5. Mr Brown also gave the following words that he could not recall on the later occasion:

There was other characters. ... The one that I mind was:
> Here comes in old Beelzebub
> And over my shoulder I carry my club.

And then the question is:
> What have you seen on your travels?

He says: Seen? Mountains o beef and rivers o gravy.

EL	Do you remember how you got your nickname?
WB	Yes, yes. It was – he was a baker's vanman. Lillicoe was his name. And it was before I went to the school, and I've been Doc Brown ever since.
EL	And was it this Lillicoe that taught you the play?
WB	Well, no. It was the rest of the boys. It was a done thing at that time. ...
EL	When was this you went round?
WB	Oh, 1913, I think.
EL	Yes.
WB	It was Christmas time; we did it at Christmas time.
EL	Was it just one night you went round?
WB	Och no, no, no. It lasted a good time at Christmas time.
EL	But would you start on Christmas?
WB	Oh well, before.
EL	Oh, before Christmas. And when did you stop?
WB	Oh well, jist New Year. It was finished at New Year. ...
EL	And these boys taught you the play?
WB	Yes, yes. Well, ye just learnt it from the older ones.
EL	Do you remember their names, that taught you?
WB	Oh, one Tom Cook and ... Jack Paterson and ... Walter Cook. ...
EL	And how did they teach you?
WB	Oh jist, ye jist went wi them and you jist heard them sayin it.
EL	Yes.
WB	Ye see, you got your bit off and that was aa that mattered.
EL	And did you have a special bit yourself?
WB	Aye, oh I'd Doctor Brown.
EL	So you went round with these boys, did you?
WB	Oh yes, yes. It was a great thing going to the door. 'Let the guisarts in!' Of course, if they didn't let you in ye asked them to assist ye. I mean, a penny was a lot in these days.
EL	Yes.
WB	Aye, aye.
EL	So how many of you went round together?

WB Oh, about four, four or five.
EL Yes. And you were always Doc?
WB I was always Doctor Brown.
EL Was that because you were Brown?
WB Yes, I think that's how I was there wi being so young, being Doctor Brown.
EL You were the youngest of them?
WB Oh mostly, mostly.
EL How old were you?
WB Oh, ten to eleven year old.
EL Yes. And how old would the others be?
WB Well, they – now they'd be getting on for fourteen, the others, or maybes a wee bit older, but I think about fourteen.
EL So you did it in 1913?
WB Ah, well, that's the last time I mind because I remember o the war startin. ...
EL Would you like to say what you remember of it?
WB The first man was Galashan.

> *Galashan*   Here comes in Galashan,
> Galashan is my name;
> A sword and pistol by my side
> I hope to win the game.
>
> *Jack*   The game sir, the game sir,
> It's not within your power;
> I'll cut ye down in inches
> In less than half an hour.
>
> *Galashan*   You, sir?
> *Jack*   I, sir.
> *Galashan*   Take yir sword and try, sir.
>
> Then they have a scrap. Jack goes down.
> *Galashan again*:
>
> See, see, what have I done?
> I've killed my father's only son.
>
> Then he looks along.
>
> Here's Doctor Brown.

Doctor Brown	Here comes in old Doctor Brown
	The best old doctor in the town.
Galashan	How much will you take to cure this man?
The Doctor	Twenty pound.
Galashan	Far too much.
Doctor Brown	Ten pound.
Galashan	Far too much.
Doctor Brown	Five pound.
Galashan	Oh, that'll do.
The Doctor	I've got a little bottle in my pocket called hoxypoxy.
	A little to his nose and a little to his toes.
	Rise up, Jack, and sing a song.

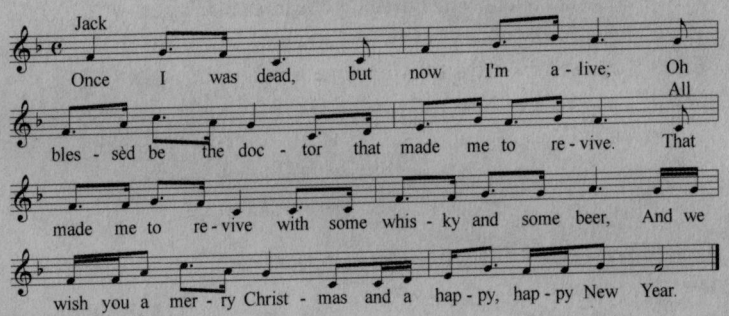

Jack: Once I was dead, but now I'm a-live; Oh All bles-sèd be the doc-tor that made me to re-vive. That made me to re-vive with some whis-ky and some beer, And we wish you a mer-ry Christ-mas and a hap-py, hap-py New Year.

Noo that's aa that I know. Bit there was other characters in it. I think a lot o them dropped out. But oh there wis more characters than that.

EL You knew some other words, didn't you?

WB Well, there was one – Who was the other one? Beelzebub or something. 'Over my shoulder I carry a club.' Ah, I can't remember it.

EL And who went round to collect the money? Did someone go round?

WB Oh well, they handed to one, but there was always a

	treasurer in the company to get the whole lot until it was split up.
EL	Yes. And what were you wearing?
WB	Oh, yer coat outside in, yer face black. No a great make-up, but trying to disguise yersel as much as possible.
EL	How did you blacken your face?
WB	Oh, jist soot or anything. ... Just blacken your face so you looked a bit different than usual.
EL	And did people have to guess who you were?
WB	Oh, they knew fine, they knew fine who we were.
EL	Did they say?
WB	No, no, they never said.
EL	And what would you wear on your head?
WB	Oh, I don't suppose we had anything on.
EL	So your coats inside out and your faces blackened –
WB	Aye, or any old thing on, ye know.
EL	And what was the fighting done with?
WB	Oh, sticks or something, anything jist to make a noise, you know.

3 Harry Fox – Morebattle, 1938–1942

I recorded Harry Fox in the school at Morebattle on 11 May 1984, and Bob Pringle, an older man, was present for the first part of the interview (SA1984.030). When I was first seeking memories of the play in Morebattle in 1979, the first door I knocked on was that of Harry's parents, Tom and Annie Fox, and this proved to be very lucky: for not only did Mr Fox immediately give me his version of the play as he had performed it about 1910–1914, but it turned out that he was a key figure in keeping the play active in the village in the next generation. The text and tune recorded from Tom Fox (SA1979.091A) were published in *Tocher* no. 32, and in Hayward, pp. 250–52.

Mrs Annie Paterson (SA1984.031B) remembered seeing the play performed with her brother Bobby as one of the actors, and knew about it having been started up again.

> This would be about 1941. '33 Robert was born and he'd be about eight or nine I think when he came in with the other boys and in the middle of the floor. They were almost unrecognisable but not quite because we knew them all so well. They had different hats and blackened faces and old trousers all different, and the doctor one had a hat and it was quite a wee thing that they did from bygone days that their father had done. And they thought, well, pity to let this go, we'll give the boys a bit briefing on it. And I think Tommy Fox was the one who really took an interest and Harry Fox was his son. And there was an age group of them, four or five of them. There was Harry Fox and Sandy Palmer, and Jimmy Nairn and Bobby I think was in it maybe once, I don't think he was in it a lot, Robert Paterson, and I think Harry took the leading part.

Harry Fox remembered all about the play and how his father taught it to them. The rather surprising lines in his version, where the Doctor speaks of carrying a club and a frying pan, were transmitted to Harry by his father, but Tom Ovens, who played the part of the Doctor in Morebattle during World War I, was aware that these lines belonged to another character who carried the club on his shoulder 'in a swaggering sort of way' (SA1984.033B). Galashin's opponent is unnamed in Harry's account, but his father called him The Game Sir, and that name has been used to introduce the speeches here. The play was still being passed on among boys into the 1920s, but there had been such a gap before Harry's time that he had never seen the play performed.

HF I cannae mind o onie other group daein a guisin act that came intae oor hoose, you know. My faither got us goin roon aboot 1937 or '38, that was when I was only nine, you see, and I did that fae aboot nine year aul roon tae aboot thirteen. ...We were going out till the beginning o the war when we were aboot thirteen or fourteen year old and you're beginnin to grow up and grow oot o that sort o thing then. Sandy [Palmer] was a wee bit aulder than me, ye see.

BP Who were the fellas?

HF Bill Scott, Jimmy Nairn, Sandy and masel. ... You see my faither and his cronies din it when they were little laddies away back in 1914 and 1912, you see, this was where it came from. ... It wis the Halloween we did it at. But there was nae reason for it bein Halloween, as I say, what we did yon time, there wis nothing aboot Halloween in it, nothing, nothing at all. But we chose to dae it then because Halloween time then was a kind of a party time. You see your Christmas time, well it was jist Christmas and New Year, ye had yer twae festive seasons there, but Halloween time was mair o a pairty time. And they held very, very big pairties in the big hooses. In Halloween time I can mind o goin oot here and watchin the firework shows in Otterburn when Mrs Pearson was there. It wis nae expense spared, she pit up thousands and thousands o huge things that we couldnae afford tae buy but we got the pleesure o watchin them, you know. She was a great lady, she was a great woman in the locality.

BP You see the only way that we used to dae that I could hae mind o was wi the cakes and that, and yon was a New Year's Day yin. On New Year's Day, you ken, you went oot and you got your bit shortbread or your cakes and in ye cam.

HF I think that some o them, especially the aulder folk, liked you to come in on New Year's Day.

BP They did. They still do.

HF Yes, they do. I've went to a few masel, even yet. But even as

	little kids they used to like you to come in and always carry a wee bit coal wi ye, aye have a bit coal in yer hand. That was good luck for them, ye see?
BP	Aye.
HF	If ye'd nothing in yer hand they would send ye back oot tae get somethin. 'Don't come in empty-handed,' ye see?
BP	Oh aye. … I can mind o ye comin in and you were the Doctor, weren't you?
HF	Doctor Brown.
BP	You were Doctor Brown. You had the hard part.
HF	Sandy was Number Three that killed Jimmy Nairn. And Jimmy came in braggin wi his dagger and his pistol.
BP	And what was Bill?
HF	Bill was Little I, 'Here comes in Little I'.
BP	Och aye. …
HF	Well Bill came in, he came in Number One, ye see, and he went to the middle of the floor and he jist:

Little I   Here comes in Little I,
　　　　　That's never been before.
　　　　　I'll try to do the best I can.
　　　　　The best can do no more.

That was his bit. And then Jimmy came in as Galashin.

Galashin   Here comes in Galashin,
　　　　　Galashin is my name.
　　　　　Wi a sword and pistol by my side,
　　　　　I hope to win the game.

And Sandy immediately barged in on *him*. And Sandy said,

The Game Sir   The game sir, the game sir,
　　　　　　It's not within your power.
　　　　　　I'll ram my dagger through your heart
　　　　　　In less than half an hour.

And Jimmy as Galashin says,

Galashin　　　You, sir?
The Game Sir　Yes, I, sir.

And Nairn,

GALOSHINS REMEMBERED

      Galashin   Take your sword and try, sir.
      Sandy jist dunted it and down fell Jimmy, see, at once on the flair. That was enter in Doctor Brown, then, ye see?

BP   And who went for Doctor Brown?

HF   Oh sorry, I beg your pardon, Sandy said a wee something then.

      The Game Sir   Oh, oh, what have I done?
                            I've killed my sister's only son.
                            Round the kitchen, round the hall,
                            Is there not a doctor to be found at all?

      That's what Sandy said, ye see? And that's when the knock at the door and Doctor Brown came in, ye see?

      Doctor Brown   Here comes in old Doctor Brown,
                            The best old doctor in the town.
                            Over my shoulder I carry a club,
                            And in my hand a frying pan.
                            And I think myself a jolly good man.

      See? Sandy immediately turned and he said,

      The Game Sir   Can ye cure a dead man?
      Doctor Brown   Yes, I can cure him.

      Ye know? And a little bottle appeared fae here, ye see? My little bottle of hoxy croxy.

      Doctor Brown   A little to his nose and a little to his toes.
                            Rise up Jack and sing a song!

      Which he promptly did.

BP   Aye. Can you mind the song he sung?

HF   When he jumped up we simply all joined hands and we sang yon little song, jist a little thing, a little bit verse that my faither made up.

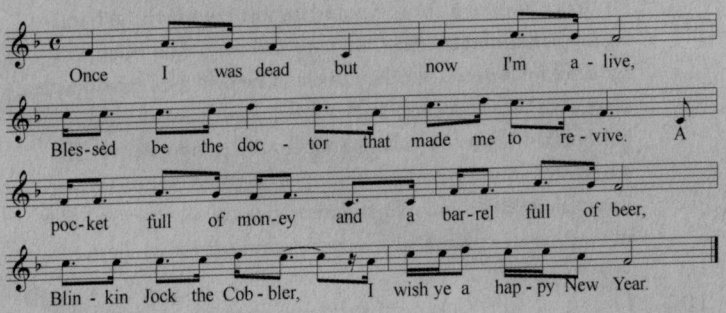

> Once I was dead but now I'm a-live,
> Bles-sèd be the doc-tor that made me to re-vive. A
> poc-ket full of mon-ey and a bar-rel full of beer,
> Blin-kin Jock the Cob-bler, I wish ye a hap-py New Year.

Ye see. That's where it might have said that it could've been a new year thing. But that's what it said. And after that Doctor Brown simply took his hat off and he said to whoever was in the room:

Doctor Brown

> Ladies and gentlemen, you'll never grow fat,
> If you don't put a penny in the old man's hat.
> If you haven't got a penny a halfpenny will do,
> But if you havenae got a halfpenny then
> God bless you.

And that's how it finished off, ye see? They always had to put a couple of ha'pennies, a couple of pennies. … They used to just divide the village, as it was then, intae fower. I mean it wis minus aa the cooncil hooses, mind you. … There's at least twenty hooses more now than there wis then. But it wis still a case of havin aboot twelve hooses per night. … That was it. Great fun! Great fun! But I mean we were always looked aifter for faither was always behind us. He never let us oot any further than twae doors in front o him, he was always in the background somewhere, jist in case. I mind one night jist at this very first hoose – the auld Foxes lived in it. They are relations of mine in a far off way. The auld man was called Bob Fox. He was a bit of a grumble in a way, he hadna much time for fun like that, and we rung the bell and got nae answer. We tried it again and got nae answer. And

Jimmy of course went forrit and he just stood wi the hand on the bell and let it ring and ring and ring. And of course the auld man dived oot the door and he'd a book. His glasses were away up here, and he'd a great, huge, egg-shaped, bald heid and wi the glasses sittin in the middle he wis like a monster. And he had a book open. And he played two or three lashes at Jimmy Nairn before he got oot the road. But my faither saw that and we got a tickin off for daein it.

BP Aye, aye.

HF I mean we were ticked off for daein that.

BP If they didnae come the first time, ye ken –

HF Ye were jist tae carry on. Needless tae say we didnae get intae that hoose, but it wis jist wan o the very few that you didnae get intae.

EL So your father was keeping an eye to see –

HF Aye he did always. After all, I don't care whae the laddies are, if you pit four laddies away for a night and it's gey funny if they don't have a wee bit argument or something or other.

BP Oh aye.

EL Oh, that's great, you really remembered the whole thing. I think maybe your father didn't tell me the last bit about the penny in the hat.

HF That was how it finished off, I mean, that's how ye came tae collect yer money. Withoot sortae begging for it, you know, ye was able to make a little bit of a poem wi it and it aa fitted in wi a little song. ... After the song ye made yer little verse for the money and that was yer programme. It was something that took, well, approximately five minutes. ... But it was quite enjoyed by everybody. And I mean the fact that people let ye in for a second and a third time, ye know, as years went on, they sorta looked forrit tae it.

EL The first year that you went round, did people say, 'It's been a little while since this has been done', or anything like that?

HF Well, yes, I think they would be a wee bit surprised, although being a thing in the village, people knew it was coming.

	Because I mean in a small village like this everybody had a fairly good idea about other people's affairs. And my father being a local worker, working in the village quite a lot, and knowing everybody, and everybody knowing him well, they would realise that he was learnin boys to do this, ye see? My father was quite keen on amateur dramatics.
EL	Oh I see, yes.
HF	So I mean it wisnae anything new for him to start telling someone how to act it and behave. There was quite a strong dramatic club in the village at that time. I can remember going to some of the plays in here and in the hall. ...
EL	Did you get your own costume together, or what happened?
HF	Well as far as the guising was concerned there wasnae really much of a costume. It was just a matter of doing a bit patchwork and a wee bit touch of black on your face, you know, just a touch of soot. My father just took a wee touch out the chimney. A wee touch on yer face, ye know.
EL	Did you have hats?
HF	Yes we aa had hats.
EL	What were they like?
HF	Well, more of the sort of the bunnet-type things there was in those days. ...
EL	What about yourself as Doctor Brown?
HF	I wore a bowler hat.
EL	Bowler was it? Yes.
HF	That was handy for the money tae!
EL	What did you do, do you remember, with the money after – It was it in your hat when you were collecting, was it?
HF	Well, after it was finished we just sortae tipped it intae wir hands and it went intae one o the big pockets in ma coat. Ye see, there was a big pocket in ma coat, and it wis taken home tae ma father's hoose and we'd count it out on the table an divide it intae four.
EL	Each evening?
HF	Oh absolutely, right down tae a ha'penny. ... And anything

else such as sweeties. That was the thing we got quite a lot of, you know. Sometimes you maybe wouldnae get any money but you would get maybe a couple of bars o chocolate, which was a great thing in those days because after all, you couldnae afford to go and buy a bar o chocolate wi yer Saturday penny, you know. Your Saturday penny went to the extent of ten sweeties or maybe one bit chewing gum and five sweeties, something like that. But to get enough to get yourself a big bar o chocolate wis something great, you know. So I mean, everything was so much appreciated.

EL So did you quite look forward to this?

HF Oh yes, it was something we looked forrit to every year. It was the same as looking forrit to school holidays, in fact. It seemed to come along that way. At that time in the schools there was no mid-term. It was during the war they started the great big mid-term holiday for gatherin potatoes, I remember, but previous to that it was jist a case of school summer holidays right up to Christmas time. So this was a sort of thing that we looked forrit to right in the middle. It wisnae school holidays, but it wis something that you looked forward to, it was something extra, ye know. ...

EL That's great, the way you remember it all.

HF Your kid's days do stick out in your mind though, at least mine do anyway. You know, right back into school time, things as happened at school, I remember very well. ...

EL If someone didn't let you in, were you annoyed?

HF No, no, because we'd been well enough told not to bother anybody. Some of the older people maybe didn't want you to come in. After all, I mean as people get older they maybe need more sleep, they were maybe no feeling too well or something like that and, 'Don't annoy anybody', that's what we were told, all the time.

EL Did any special one of you knock at the door?

HF Well I think usually the Number One, Little I, did the knocking. We jist sortae went to the door in proper rotation. Little

I knocked at the door and whoever answered the door, you see, 'Will you let the guisers act?' That was what he said. ... That was the request made and they would either say 'Yes' or 'No', which was 'Yes' in I would say ninety-five per cent of cases.

EL Yes. Oh that's all very clear. Oh well, I think the boys here are going to learn it up, some of the schoolchildren.

HF Well, it would be nice to see somebody else do it. I mean this is forty-five years on and I've never seen anybody else do it in front of me, and I'd like to see four laddies do it, I really would, I'd like to see it. ...

EL What about the others of you besides the Doctor, what were they wearing?

HF Well, it was a case of having maybe one of your dad's coats on, you know, just to sort of get the schoolboy image away fae ye. So ye'd get yin o yer dad's coats on. No to the extent of being sort o like a uniform or anything like that; I mean, people knew who ye were, ye werenae sorta disguised oot o sight aatogether. My dad, he used his finger and he just put a wee bit black ower yer eyes and maybe a bit touch on yer chin, you know.

EL He made you up?

HF He made you up as he wanted it and it was possibly more than likely what happened to them when they were laddies. ...

EL Yes. And did you, when you had this aspirin bottle, did you uncork it or unscrew the top?

HF It was a screw top, one of the tiny wee screw tops.

EL I thought you were doing a screw motion! ... You were saying about the swords. ...

HF Yes. Well, I mean the sword bit came when Number Three came in and said:

> The game sir, the game sir,
> It's not within your power.
> I'll ram my dagger through your heart

>In less than half an hour.
>
>And then Jimmy said (Number Two, Galoshin) he said,
>>You, sir?
>
>Number Three said,
>>Yes, I, sir.
>
>And he said immediately,
>>Take your sword and try, sir.
>
>And before he could do anything, Number Three had took his sword out and done it. So ye see, when he dropped to the floor his sword was still tangled up in his clothes, ye see?

EL   So it was quite a small, a short sword, almost a dagger sort of length, was it?

HF   It was just, they were just made wi wood. They werenae – there was nothing dangerous about them – they werenae even real daggers, they were just made out of wood intae a wooden dagger.

EL   Kind of a stick?

HF   It was jist, wi a wee cross on it.

EL   A cross-piece, yes. So it was just a single stabbing movement?

HF   Yes, that was it, a touch there, a touch.

EL   In the stomach, was this?

HF   Aye, yes. And instead o falling intae a heap, and he did fall down, ye know he got himself nice and straight out so that I could get the bottle to his nose and his toes. I think it made quite a bigger sort of impression when he actually got up that he was lying full-length, you know, he had to go through the whole motion of rolling around and getting up on to his feet again.

EL   Yes, that's very vivid!

HF   But it was funny in a way. Because I can remember in the sorta last years that we did it, when you went intae a hoose and there was children watching, when this bit took place and the boy fell to the floor, there were some wee gasps of amazement fae children, naturally, in the hoose, because I mean this was actually happenin in front o their eyes, ye see.

	I mean it wis all in fun, but then a kiddie wasnae to know that, ye see? Kids o eight or nine year auld, I mean this was something terrible to happen in their house.
EL	So they really thought –
HF	So I mean they were thinking, 'Oh my goodness, what are we seeing here?' But of course it was all joy in a few minutes because he was back up on his feet again.
EL	Yes, that's great. So they really took it in seriously.
HF	If ye can imagine yersel as a child, if somebody was to sorta take a dagger and down somebody right in front of you.
EL	Where he lay straight flat out! Oh well. And so he jumped up and he's singing?
HF	Oh, he sings too, yes, everybody sings at the end.
EL	You all sing that song?
HF	Everybody sings that song at the very end. It was quite a noisy chorus wi four laddies as you can imagine.
EL	Yes! I wonder how long it had stopped before you restarted it? …
HF	It must have been a fair bit before because, as I said before, I cannae remember anybody comin intae the house doin an act of any kind. …
EL	Did you say you were asked to do the play in a concert hall one time?
HF	In the village hall, oh aye.
EL	When was that, what sort of event was that?
HF	Oh that could have been the very late thirties, '39, maybe '40.
EL	The village hall?
HF	In the village hall because they were having a function as they did every year of course. As I say the dramatic society, they had something going every year. …
EL	Yes.
HF	And there again, as I say there was no television, no other form of amusement so I mean people just came in there, it was the same with dances. … I sit and watch telly an awful

lot but it's jist a new way o life, really. I think I can look back and remember playin dominoes and whist wi ma auld grandfather [Henry Fox, Tommy Fox's father] in the hoose. I enjoyed that as a schoolkid, you know, I think.

EL Did your grandfather ever talk about this play? ...

HF No, I cannae remember him saying anything aboot that. And I mean I was eleven when he died, so I'd have remembered if he had said anything.

EL Yes, well.

HF But he was always quite pleased to see the boys in the hoose hissel. Usually we were in ma father's hoose maybe, oh, three or four nights and we would try it oot twice, at least four nights before we were turn't ontae the street. Ye see, it wasnae a case of jist gettin thegither and goin away and doin this thing, no, no. He had to have us in the hoose and, 'We'll go through this again' and he'll put us back out and 'Ye'll come in again and let's see you do it better this time'. And he wouldnae let you away until ye had it off perfect. He believed in having it right.

EL You said I think – did you write it down yourself?

HF I wrote the words doon ... Dad had them written down originally for us to read. We all got our little bit poem to read and learn. ...

EL So your father wrote out the different parts, did he?

HF Away back, yes, when we started, right at the very start. Just to get – each one of the four got their bit to read and to memorise, just like doing a wee play.

EL So he rehearsed you up.

HF And then we never needed it again after we got it the first time. We just went to a coupl'a houses and that was it. We'd just never forget it. And I'm quite sure that the other three lads'll can remember their bit as well now as they did yesterday. ... I think we would do it until aboot – well I'm only gaun for my own age – see we stopped doin it at fourteen so that was '43, we would actually do it, 1942 would

	be our last year. I think so. … I think we would do it aboot four or five year, until '42.
EL	'42 was your last one. And then it was when you left school you stopped?
HF	It was when we left school, well then ye sorta get off these things, don't you.
EL	And you never did it after you left school?
HF	We never did it after that, no.
EL	This Otterburn one was while you were still at school?
HF	Oh yes, that was during the very, very early war I would think, 1939 maybe. But it was a great night doon there, a typical Mrs Pearson party. A tremendous thing! But it was strange walking, I mean you're talking aboot the war days and when ye were goin doon there ye were walkin in pitch dark, there was no lights whatever and ye couldnae even put a torch on or ye had the local bobby on yer top, ye see, for showin the light, you know. We had to make our way for a mile along the road there and there's quite a small road entailed in that. But being local laddies we knew aa the road wursel and it was a great night. …
EL	What was it you were saying about your normal size of audience in a normal room?
HF	Well jist take an ordinary village and an ordinary family. And an ordinary family if ye could just say a mother and a father and two of a family, maybe three, maybe four sometimes, but I mean that's about right, ye know, a mother, a father, a couple o kids and maybe a grandfather or a granny. Five would be an average sorta company that you would do it in front o. Sometimes you were jist doin it tae one. I mean some old person living themselves and I think they in turn would just love to get ye intae the house for a wee bit company, just a wee bit company, ye know. And they would lavish ye wi bags o chocolate, toffee and that. Auld ladies in particular. We had an auld couple, a couple of auld ladies in the village at one time called the Miss Tullys. They were a

great pair because they did love to have this in their house, ye see, and there was only two o them but, oh dear, they lavished things ontae ye. ... They lived in Yarradoon. ... There wis other big houses such as the doctor in those days. The village doctor lived in Mainsfield. ... When ye went intae the living room in Mainsfield or in Yarradoon it wis a huge place, ye know. Yir furniture wis – ye had plenty room, ye had too much room sometimes. Ye had to compare that wi next door which had a tiny little room. So ye did yir little act in aa kinds o places.

EL Did you adapt it a bit, depending on this?

HF Well, not really, jist if there wis more room than ye were sortae used to, well I mean there wis more room to do the little act in. But I think preferably the lot o us would jist like to do it in an ordinary kitchen, an ordinary living room.

EL There'd often be a fire, I suppose?

HF Always a fire, always, absolutely because as I say there was practically no electricity in those days, ye see. Ye were daein this act in paraffin heatin and paraffin lighting aa the time, the auld paraffin lamp on the table. Or the tilly on the wall, no the tilly, what did we call the other one again? The auld Aladdin lamp. And then there was the other one that stuck in the wall. ... They had it on the mantelpiece and it was paraffin, the sort o thing that my auld relatives had and it was forever goin up if ye were too busy readin or havin a game o dominoes. You felt the wee smell and when ye turned round the mantle was aa blackened and ye turned it off for a wee while, and then ye got nothing left but the flicker o the coal, the flame in the fire. But everything was so homely somehow, ye know, ye were really daein it jist in a home. Everything was just simple, everything so simple.

EL Where were you placed in relation to the fire then, when you were acting it?

HF Well, I think everybody's hoose, in those days in particular, the fire was what ye all sat round aboot, the furniture was round about the fire. So if people made room for ye they simply pushed a chair or maybe a sofa back from the fire so ye were doin it almost always in front of it or quite close to it. That's the general way o a house as I knew it. And it's the way o ma house yet, because I've still got a fire and most o the village houses've got a fire too, and that's their central place, you know. I'm always a wee bit bamboozled when ye go intae these new houses where there's no fire, jist, I wonder where people sit in here? What can ye sit round aboot? A fire seems tae make a place. You use that as something that you sit round about.

EL Well, it certainly made a good acting area.
HF Aye, lovely.

4 Michael Crosby – Hawick, 1950–1955 and 1991–1996

Along with Laurie Romanosky, I recorded Michael Crosby and his wife Edith at their home near Linlithgow on 29 June 1996 (SA1996.065). Laurie was a student in the School of Scottish Studies working on a study of 'Hallowe'en in Scotland Past and Present' for her MLitt degree, and I suggested that it would be interesting to try to trace some knowledgeable people through a local newspaper and to include a request for information about *Galoshins*. We settled on West Lothian, and Laurie wrote a letter that was published in *The Linlithgowshire Journal and Gazette*. The only response relating to *Galoshins* came from Michael Crosby, who knew a Borders, not a West Lothian, tradition of the play. He recalled taking part in it as a boy at the home of his grandmother, Mrs Isabella (Bella) Crosby, in Hawick, and he had taught it to his two sons and had been performing it with them in Hawick in the year of recording. He had never heard of the play outside this family context. The opponent of Galatians was named Horatio and they called the play by this name.

EL　Well, you know this *Galoshins* play. How do you know about it?

MC　The play was traditionally done at the New Year by my father and he passed it on to his three children ... which is a nice number for doing the play because the play has three people in it. And it was traditionally done every New Year when we went down to visit our granny as the family always used to convene on New Year's Day for a family get-together.

EL　On New Year's Day then, not Hogmanay?

MC　Not Hogmanay; it was actually New Year's Day that we went down, yes.

EL　What time of day?

MC　You'd be down for about mid-day and have afternoon tea there and all the aunts and uncles would convene as well.

EL　Well, I'd be interested in just everything about it, you know.

MC　Clearly, in those days, the whole family, the extended family used to live relatively near. One or two aunts or uncles lived out of the town, but not many. And they'd all convene on New Year's Day. Granny, being head of the ... family, ... she would organise the day and the meal. There'd be little things like lucky dips which were made up for all the children. You were expected to go into, I guess it would be a shopping basket, and little gifts were wrapped up and you'd stick your hand in and [get] a small gift of very little value because I guess in those days the grandparents had very little money at all, so very small silly gifts ... stupid things like a box of matches. Father smoked and he had to guddle about in the bottom of the bag to find the one that rattled so that he could get the gift. Each one of the family would be expected to do a little – what's the word? – a little song and dance or a little –

EC Would you call it a turn?
MC Yes, a little turn and the Crosby family would do *Galatians* and ... the three of us fitted the parts correctly. My eldest sister [Ann] would do Galatians, my middle sister [Ruth] would do Horatio. We had a huge problem remembering the name of Horatio because it's not in the play. It's a good word for the play that never mentions Horatio at all! And I was the young one so I got the smallest part which was Doctor Brown.
EL You might just like to run it through.
MC OK, I'll try and do it but you're meant to sing it at the end which I don't know if I will or not. So here it goes. I don't know how I'll do the different parts but:

Galatians	Here steps in Galatians,
	Galatians is my name;
	With sword and pistol by my side,
	I hope to win the game.
Horatio	The game sir, the game sir,
	'Tis not within your power;
	I'll slash you and bash you
	Within half an hour.
Galatians	You, sir?
Horatio	I, sir.
Galatians	Well take your sword and try, sir.

And then you have a little sword fight where Horatio is dramatically killed and there's a call that says:

Galatians   Is there a doctor in the house?

And in I come.

Doctor Brown   Here in steps old Doctor Brown
The greatest doctor in all the town;
With a pinch to your toes and a pinch to your nose;
Rise up young man and give us a song.

And then all people join in, although it should just be Horatio does it, but everybody joins in. So it's:

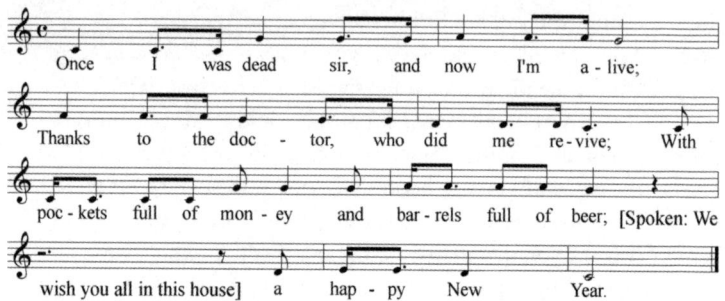

Once I was dead sir, and now I'm a-live; Thanks to the doctor, who did me revive; With pockets full of money and barrels full of beer; [Spoken: We wish you all in this house] a happy New Year.

To all great applause from the aunts and uncles who thought it was wonderful. ...

EL   And how were you all dressed?

MC   We were actually in smart clothes. You weren't actually dressed up for the play *per se,* but it was the family get-together, so everybody was in Sunday best or whatever for that.

EL   Did your father talk about how he used to do it?

MC   We've drawn a complete blank on where or how this had come. I spoke to my mother, spoken to my eldest remaining aunt. They don't know where that came from, at all. So we can't actually link when my father first got it . ... We've done it since I was five, and so that takes you back to the early 50s, and clearly my father did it long before that as well. ...

EL   And you said, I think, ... that he taught you it?

MC   Yes, basically he taught us it and my big sister and the other sister, they learned it quite quickly, but I must have been very young when I got it because what they did for me was they got a bit of paper with four lines or whatever it is written on it, so the fact that I couldn't remember four lines indicates that I was quite small at the time. And what they did was every time we went through it and scored out another word until eventually I had a bit of paper that had everything scored out and I knew it by then.

EL   Did he tell you how to do the actions? …

MC   I think basically the play was done by my elder sisters and him before I got involved and by then I had seen it done by him as being Doctor Brown and I just replaced him. So it cycled in through that and like yes, it was very much dramatised actions, you know, the sword fight and the pinch to your nose, pinch to your toes. So it was quite exaggerated.

EL   So what did you actually do when you –? Did you stand to one side? I know it's a very little thing to remember, but –

MC   No, no. Basically, you have, Galatians steps in – well Horatio is already there and Galatians steps in and he says, 'Here steps in Galatians', then obviously Horatio throws down the challenge. And the sword fight happens, very dramatised, he dies. Then I walk in to Horatio's side. Facing the audience so you can pinch the toes, pinch the nose, then 'Rise up young man and give us a song'. Then the three of you line up and sing the song. Again, it's dramatised actions, you know. 'Thanks to the doctor who did me revive. With pockets full of money, and barrels full of beer; We wish you all in this house a happy New Year.' So it's good for the kids, the kids can actually do the actions and things like that.

EL   So you were doing a few actions there. Can you just describe them?

MC   OK. So basically when you've said about 'pinch to the toes, pinch to the nose', there were very dramatised touching of the toes and nose. Then when you do the song, you line up as a group together, as a friendly group, because you're all lined up in line and all happy. And you say, when you say 'With pockets full of money', you slap your thighs or your hip pockets. 'And barrels full of beer' you actually swig almost like a beer glass, which is a bit perverse because that's nothing to do with barrels. But 'We wish you all in this house a happy New Year', and when they say 'Thanks to the doctor', you do a flourish to the doctor with your hand, thanking him.

EL   And immediately after it was over, there was applause?

MC   Applause, yes.

EL   Did they give you anything at that point?

MC   I don't think so, because I think all, the only gifts that were done was this lucky draw. ...

EL   What were the weapons?

MC   There were two swords. We clearly, well, did we actually have swords with us? No. You probably just dramatised the swords, so as I say, it was all made up and –

EL   You mean, you think they were just imagined?

MC   Yeah, well like the swords, you pretended to have a sword fight but you didn't actually physically have the swords.

EL   So you just flourished your hand?

MC   Yes, that's right. ...

EL   Where exactly was this? ...

MC   We lived in Burnfoot, in Hawick, which was in those days a brand new housing scheme, and my granny lived in Northcote Street, in Hawick, right in the town centre, in a tenement. ... I don't think there's any specific songs for Halloween that we did, but, like New Year, there were some things that we had, jokes and things like that, that are specific to New Year ... There's 'Get up auld wife'. Now that's what we used to go round to my granny's – and you'd go and knock on the door and say:

> Get up auld wife, and shake your feathers,
> Dinna think that we are beggers,
> We're only bairns come oot to play,
> Get up and gie's our Hogmanay.

and you'd get, you know, fruit or whatever gift, then.

EL   When was that you went round?

MC   Hogmanay, in the morning.

EL   So the morning of the last day of the year?

MC   That's right, that's when you got sent along the high street to look for the man with as many noses as there's days in the year, as well. So all us kids were going along looking for people with lots of noses, but not realising there's only one day left in the year! ...

EC   I don't know if that's just my dad but he – It's

> Hogmanay, Hogmanick,
> Hing the butcher ower the stick,
> Gie him yen, gie him twa,
> Knock his heid agin the wa. ...

It's just one of the things he taught us when we were little.

EL   Did you do anything special with it? Did you say it at any special time?

EC   No, we just said it on Hogmanay, and again, he used to send us along to the end of the street to watch for this man with all the noses, you know, you could be standing along the end of the street for half an hour or an hour waiting for this man, you know! ...

MC   In England they say New Year's Eve and in Scotland we say Old Year's Night. ...

EC   I rarely call it Hogmanay.

EL   You'd call it Old Year's Night, yes?

EC   Yes.

EL   Now you were saying that you were doing it with your son – back to *Galoshins* again.

MC   That's right, yes.

EL   So tell me a bit about that.

MC   Well, it's just as you try and carry on traditions. What we've typically done is that, since we've got married, we've tried to keep Christmas to ourselves and we tend to have Christmas here as a family event but still go back down to the Borders for New Year and same sort of thing that we tend not to have a big formal do with the family there, do we, on New Year's Day now, but we still make sure that the children do their party pieces. Only having two kids, clearly I have to step into the breech. ... So my older son who's thirteen now, he does Galoshins, I'm Horatio because I get killed, and the little one, who's ten now, he does Doctor Brown. And he's done it since he was tiny because he couldn't say 'the greatest doctor', he said 'the wonderfullest doctor in the whole town' and he used to take great joy in pinching my nose, with a nice big twist at the same time!

5 Wat Ramage – Westruther, 1914–1917

Wat Ramage performed in the play at Hogmanay in the village of Westruther, near Lauder, and, when first recorded in 1977, said it was 'away aboot sixty years ago anyway'. He went round with the other children who lived in his row, and in a 1984 interview he said: 'I was at Westruther School and stoppit at a farm at Thornydykes. There were six houses. We used to start at the top and do them aa, ye ken. ... It was aa wir ain folk, the bairns oot o each hoose and they was aa joined thegither. ... And we got aa our cakes into the baskets, ye see.' I recorded him three times at his home in Hounam, near Morebattle (SA1977.205, SA1979.091, SA1984.035A) and extracts from all three recordings are given here. Mr Ramage was a shepherd, and published his own life story, *An Auld Herd's Memories*, in 1983. He was a fiddle player and a singer and recalled the song very clearly, but the words as a whole came back to him only gradually. His full play text has been put together from different points in the 1984 interview.

1977

EL   You were remembering going round at Hogmanay. Could you tell me a bit about that? ...

WR   They got all dressed up, ye see, bairns ... they went to the door and knockit at the door ... and they got their cakes and things and maybe a cup o tea, and away they went to the next hoose, and jist roond first yin and then another.

EL   How far would you travel when you did this sort of thing?

WR	Oh, we didna traivel, ye ken, we didna gang that far fir there were ay another gang farther on, ye ken, daein the ither yins. ...
EL	Do you remember what people were wearing? You say they were dressed up, but what sort of clothes?
WR	Well, the laddies was maistly dressed up in the women's claes, and the lassies was dressed up in the boys' claes, an some o they old-fashioned skirts that their mothers used to wear, trailing on the ground.
EL	So it was lassies as well?
WR	Aye, aye, aye, oh aye. There was baith boys and lassies.

1979

WR	When we wis bairns at the school we had this play, *Galoshins*, and aboot a dizzen o us got dressed up at night, what we caad guisin and us guisers, and we went fae one house tae another and we had this play that we – a little play that we went through, and it wis: We went to the door and rapped at the door and when the wife came to the door we said: 'Get up auld wife and shake your feathers' ... . And then we mairched in. And after that there were another one left ahint, Galoshin, and here he landed in wi 'Here comes in Galoshin' ... . And there's one steps forrit oot o the circle and says 'The game sir, the game sir' ... . But he drew his sword an Galoshin was supposed to be dead – he fell down dead – and then there was one sent away ootside and he brought in old Doctor Brown, the best old doctor in the town, an he doctert up Galoshin, gied him some potion, an then Galoshin banged up to his feet and startit. Here's: 'Once I was dead, sir, but now I am alive' [*etc.*]. An then we went away tae anither hoose, an went from yin hoose to another, an this play went on aa night. ...
EL	Did you say the boys dressed as girls and the girls dressed as boys?

WR	Aye, aye, that's right. And your faces was blackened, ye see.
EL	How did you blacken your faces?
WR	Oh soot, just a pickle soot, just a pickle soot. Ye rubbit it on. It took a lot o washin off, I can tell ye. ….
EL	So were you standing round in a circle?
WR	Aye, oh aye, standin round in a circle.
EL	Did you move about at all?
WR	Aye, we'd be goin roond about.
EL	You were moving round in a circle, walking round?
WR	Aye, aye. … 'Aa the little bairnies that roond the table go', ye ken.
EL	Yes. And were you circling round *all* the time?
WR	Aa the time. Aye.
EL	From when you went into the house?
WR	Aye, we just joined hands, ye ken, and then roond aboot, ye see. And this yun startit forward into the middle of the ring and challenged, Here come I Galoshin, ye see, to fight. He came in and he was going to fight and this yun went into the ring and challenged him. Then had to send oot for Doctor Brown.
EL	And Doctor Brown was outside?
WR	Aye, he was ootside.
EL	But Galoshin and the other fighter were both in the ring?
WR	They were in the ring and he had a sword in his hand – they baith had swords, ye see. He stabbed him and Galoshin fell, ye see, and then after the doctor gied him some o his potion he got up to his feet and started to sing a song. …
EL	What did you do with the money you got?
WR	Oh, it wasna very hard to spend aa the money that we got! There werena much spare money in they days, I can tell you.
EL	Did it go in the baskets? Did the money go in the baskets?
WR	No, no, the money went into your pockets. Ye got a halfpenny apiece for each yin, ye ken. Oh, you just spent it at the skuil the next day.
EL	On what sort of things?

WR	Oh, just aa the sweeties that you aye got maist o for a ha'penny, aye. …
EL	And did every house want you to come in?
WR	Oh aye, we went to them aa. Ye's whiles get mair in some houses as in other yins, ken, depend on the circumstances. I'd be about ten or eleven year old.
EL	Did you go round several years, you yourself?
WR	Oh aye, I was into it every year. I'd start when I were about eight year old.
EL	And would it be half boys and half girls?
WR	Aye, well, whatever was there.
EL	It was just a mix?
WR	It was just a mixed crowd.

1984

All
Get up auld wife and shake your feathers,
Dinna think that we are beggars,
We're only bairnies come to play,
Get up and gie's wir Hogmanay.

Galoshin
Here comes in Galoshins,
Galoshin is my name,
My sword and pistol by my side,
I hope to win the game.

The other one
The game sir, the game sir,
It's not within your power
Or I could cut you down with my broadsword
Within a half an hour.

And of course they drew their swords then and something, 'Galoshin he lay dead' – 'And wi a thrust to his broadsword, Galoshin he was dead.'
And this yin says:

The other one
Horrible, horrible, what have I done?
I've killed my father's youngest son.

> Run oot as hard as ye can oot through
>   the town
> And fetch in old Doctor Brown
> The best old doctor in the town.

And Doctor Brown came in.

> *Doctor Brown*   Here comes in old Doctor Brown
>   The best old doctor in the town.

And he got into his pocket and liftit this bottle.

> A little to his nose and a little to his toes.
> Rise up, Jack, and sing a song.

> Once I was dead, sir, but now I am a-live,
> Bles-sèd be the doc-tor that made me to re-vive. Bless'd
> be the mis-tress of the house, the mas-ter al-so, And
> all the lit-tle bairn-ies that roond the ta-ble go. Wi their
> poc-kets fu o mo-ney an their bas-kets fu o gear, Suc-
> cess in-til our guis-in, a hap-py, guid New Year.

6   *Peter Thomson – Biggar, 1925–1928*

The Biggar play was exceptional in being tied in with the two rival Hogmanay bonfires built by the boys respectively of the top of the town (where Peter Thomson lived) and of the Westrow. Neill Martin, in an insightful study entitled 'A Game of Two Halves: Guising and Contest in Scotland', has suggested that the ritual rivalry just at the one time of year can be connected symbolically with the *Galoshins* fight between the warriors which ends in reconciliation and general harmony. The Westrow bonfire which was built on a hill beside the burn that formed the boundary between the two territories was especially vulnerable to attack, as Mr Thomson's account indicates. The integrated events in Biggar began some weeks after the November Fair and ended when the huge fires burnt out, which might be some days into the new year. The scale of the operation meant that the play had high visibility in the community, and after World War II Brian Lambie created a composite text and was successful in organising a revival of the play in connection with the one remaining bonfire which is still lit at the 'top of the town' on Hogmanay. The play took on a new lease of life and has been presented in a variety of forms over the years.

Mr Lambie introduced me to Peter Thomson among others, and he was present at this interview which took place on 9 July 1982 at Mr Thomson's home in Biggar (SA1982.124B, 125). Mr Lambie questioned Mr Thomson particularly about who spoke the line 'Aye, here he's, here he's, here he's', since he had heard from Bobby Moore and Mrs Elizabeth Graham (*née* Brown) that the whole group chorused this together (SA1982.124A). Mr Lambie's father's shop, where the boys bought lamps, was an ironmonger's.

Mr Thomson speaks at the start of bringing roots down for the bonfire and Sandy Robertson explains more fully what was involved (SA1982.126B):

> We used to go out just as a gang o lads, you would meet for the gathering, that's what we used to call – 'We're going gaithering the nicht,' that was it! 'We're going gaithering the nicht.' ... I've seen us up the wee hill behind us here called Bizzieberry. I've seen us go up to the old woods – you know, they had been cut down in previous years – an digging out the roots, an digging out the roots, digging the old tree roots to put onto the fire.

PT   We just sort of got together, a crowd of lads. There were two bonfires, of course, there were two bonfires as Brian will tell you. We were what you call the tap o the toon an this was mainly to collect money, well no only to buy the coal but you bought paraffin to keep the fire burnin. Plus the fact that ye had a wee divvy, and there was a gentleman would look efter aa this money an mostly in ma day it was Cocky Moore, wee Cocky Moore, and he looked after the money and on Hogmanay Night ye aa got yer wee divvy. It depended on how many nights ye had attended, how much ye got, like, for collecting wood for the fire, like. We used to go up to the Bizzieberry wood and used to bring the roots down on an old cart. Oh, we'd some marvellous times! I would say on an average maybe about fourteen boys ranging from what? about ten to fourteen – fourteen would be about the oldest, I would think. And then about a fortnight or three weeks prior to the actual fire being lit, we went out guisin, or as we caad it siguisin, we called it siguisin, why we don't know, but that's what we always caad it. And you went from the range of Skirling, Spittal, Blackwood, they call it, the Public Park, and that was about your limit, an Langlees, and that was about your limit o the boundary. I do believe the Westraw boys, they went out as far as Coulter an that kin o bit, but I don't know whether that was true or no, ken. The West Row had a fire. ...

BL   Did you poach on their –

PT   Oh, quite often!

BL   Did you go to the same places as they were going?

PT   Aye, aye. Ye slipped oot to Netherton Hoose, Biggar Park, and those places, that's what they caa the bottom o the toon places, but we did that an many a fight we had, many a good ficht we had, actually! And then of course, another thing what we did, we'd raid their bonfire, ye see, or throw it into the burn, push it doon the hill into the burn. And they would light ours, sometimes it was lit prior to the actual – twice to

	my knowledge it was lit, aye. I think once it was, what? three o'clock in the afternoon and the other time it was six at night, the actual fire was lit.
EL	The other side lit it?
PT	Deliberately. And then another thing we did, we used to get yon finnan haddies an yon smokies and, ye ken, [from] Auld Lawrie the fishman – cos he wouldna be able to keep them ower the long holiday – an we could buy them for a penny, ye ken, an ye smoked them, roasted them at the fire along wi tatties and that, some guid feeds. I've seen me no goin home till two or three in the morning and it was as black as the Earl of Hell's waistcoat tee! …
EL	Did you start doing the play then before Christmas?
PT	Aye, we started roughly – November – it was aye aboot – November we started the collecting for the fire after the fair and I would say maybe about a fortnight or three weeks after that we actually started collecting for the money and go round all the houses. And ye jist opened the door, well, you knocked, but you jist opened the door and walked straight in in most places, except the big houses, you know, ye were a wee bit, maybe a wee bit scared o doin that kind of thing. I've seen us get – at Netherlee ye got a pound, which was a lot o money in these days, but we'd all to do something. Every boy had to do something. …
EL	Did you do something as well as the play? …
PT	Oh, aye. We did the actual, ye ken, 'A room, a room' …, and then you had your own bits o poetry and wee odds and sods of rhymes:

> Mary had an iron coo,
> She milked it wi a spanner.
> The milk cam oot in shilling tins
> An wee tins for a tanner.

This kind of thing; you did a lot of wee daft kin o things, you know. But you had to do something. And then, well, usually it was a lum hat, you ken, the old tile hat, and the man went roon and collected the money in it. And then of course it was taken straight – once you'd come home to Biggar, which was maybe about half-past ten at night – ye would go straight to Cocky Moore's an ye handed in the money. Funnily enough, nobody ever cheated, you never thought o cheatin. Maybe an old person would gie you a couple of apples or something, you know, and you soon scoffed them. But oh, we'd some grand nichts. And I played, well I wisna very good, but I remember getting an old – I think there were ten buttons on it, either eight or ten buttons on the one side and so many buttons on the other, one of the old accordions, and you used to go wi that. And there were a fellow, Sanny Robinson, had a wee concertina. Sanny was guid, he was quite musical, o course. ...

EL What age were you?

PT I would be aboot maybe ten till fourteen. You see I was of a big family and my brother John had done it, and I don't know about Alec and Jimmy, but I know John and Alan had done it, so obviously I must have started about tenish, ye know, and went out until I left school. I thought I was a big boy when I left the school. I left the school at fourteen, and you stopped sort o doing it after that. ... But there were another thing, you always got extra money, remember, for the tarrin. You got sixpence for doing the tarrin o the bonfire! ...

BL Oh aye.

EL What was that, sorry?

PT For tarrin. Putting the tar on the actual bonfire and you wore all your old clothes, you know, everything that your mother was going to throw out, aa your rags, and you climbed up to the bonfire and you poured all the tar over it you got from the gasworks and some state ye got into, I can tell you, and then ye'd go home and your mother would rub butter into your hair. We were wild wee devils, when I think o it!

EL	When you blackened your faces for the play, what did you blacken them with?
PT	A cork, with the cork and a candle, you know.
EL	I'm not sure how you did that. So that was –?
PT	A cork. Ye got the old candle, and you light a candle and, ye see – and it was either a whisky cork or one o thae wine corks, some of the old-fashioned corks – every bottle had corks in thae days – and you just held it over and kept turning it on the flame – slightly above the flame – the actual cork wasn't burnin but the candle – I don't know if you know but slightly above a candle you get a little what we caa reek, you know, the black smoke, and if you held it down and you get a right – and this is what you blackened yersel wi. The cork actually semi-burnt, partial sort of charcoal, sort o charred. I think there were only one, the Moor, whoever acted the Moor, he was the only one who was really black. The rest o us simply had fancy moustaches and fancy beards an that. You never had any other what I would caa adornments, as regards false moustaches or anything like that, it was all done with the cork. Ye maybe had stripes up and doon the way, you know, something like the kinda Indian style. ...
EL	Which was the Moor? ...
PT	I don't remember what he said, actually.
BL	Would that be the Turkish Knight?
PT	I believe it was, aye, the Turkish Knight. That's aa that I can remember, but I think Alan was much better in his version. ... Sometimes their mothers didna allow them oot. You see, in fact, I'll be honest wi you, quite often Alan and I slipped oot. It was efter ye was ootside, ye turned yer jacket ootside in. ... And you made your own home-made wooden swords and you made your own shields, and aa they kinna daft things, ye know. And the club was just a great big muckle – sawn off a tree.
EL	Who had the club?

PT   Oh, Beelzebub. An then he carried a frying pan, an auld iron – by jings they were heavy some o the old frying pans, they werena the aluminium ones. Everyone did something. I've seen aboot ten o us gaun out. …

EL   How did you organise this quite long period of time really? How did you decide where you were going to start?

PT   Funnily enough, ye always had a leader and quite often I was the leader. I just seemed to have a kind o knack for it. You know, we'll go to Heavieside tonight and from Heavieside we'll go to Spittal big house and from Spittal big house we'll go to Skirling big house – you know the kind of thing – and come back in and do Coulter's Close, the MacDonalds were in at that time. And you did that one night – maybe did about four big houses plus so much o Skirling village. And then you would slip out and do Coulter village unknown to the Westraw yins – you know, this kin o thing. …

EL   Did you go into all the houses in Biggar, say?

PT   I would say we'd go into most o them in the top o the town anyway. Not so many o them in the bottom o the town.

EL   That was the Westrow one?

PT   Aye, the Westraw. We wouldna go to many there, though we did do occasionally. … But I would say mostly at the top o the town, and the top o the town stretched from – you could only go down the length of R. B. Marr's, the Municipal Hall, and that was you finished; after that, you know, that was taboo or supposed to be anyway. …

EL   What sort of fights did you have?

PT   Oh, fist fights, real fist fights, oh they were real fist fights.

EL   Did they draw blood?

PT   Oh aye, quite often, quite often. But ye just got up and carried on.

EL   Did you fight these boys at any other time of year?

PT   Oh, no, no, no. No, no, no. Oh, no. Ye didna actually – In fact ye went out to the Clyde, swimmin. … Biggar was a great wee place! … I mean everybody knew everybody, and

	yet you didna know everybody, if you understand what I mean. You know you sort o helped each other and yet ye didna sort o interfere much. ...
EL	Were you ever in Brian's revival?
BL	Alan was in it. I don't think you were ever in it.
PT	No, I was never in it. Alan was in it. ...
EL	When were you doing this, what years? ...
PT	I'd be about thirteen, twelve. I would do it from about ten year old, so that would be – 1925 I'd start it, roughly. ... I'll tell you who the first person we did it wi, Tommy Moore. Well, he stayed, ken, at the top of the town, an he was a kind o relative of Cocky's and it was through him, ye ken. He kind of showed us how tae dae it, my brother Alan and John. ...
EL	Well, ... you might like to take the play through?
PT	Well, I'll take it through as best as I know how. ...

Room	A room, a room, a gallant room,
	A room tae let us in.
	Steer up the fire an gie us a licht
	For in this hoose they'll be a ficht.
	If you don't believe these words I'll say
	I'll call in King George tae clear the way.
The MC	And who are you sir?
King George	Who am I?
	Here am I King George
	The Great King of Macedonia
	Who conquered all the world aroond
	Until he came to Scotland.
	For when he came to Scotland
	His hert grew cold
	Tae see such a little nation
	So frank, so free and so bold.
MC	And who are you sir?
Sir William Wallace	
	Who am I?

	Here am I, Sir William Wallace the noble knicht
	Who fought for Scotland's richt and Scotland's reason.
MC	And what can ye dae?

Sir William Wallace

    I can ficht man.

    I can ficht for Scotland, sir.

MC   Here are two warriors going tae ficht

    That never focht before.

    I place ma sword atween them baith

    And whit can I do mair?

    Ficht on, ficht on my merry men.

    Ficht on wi aa thy speed.

    I'll give ony man ten thoosand punds

    That kills King George stone deid.

King George and Sir William battle a wee while, you see, and then King George falls tae the flair and William Wallace says,

Sir William Wallace

    Good heavens what's this I've done?

    Killed George my faither's only son.

    Is there no a doctor in the toon?

MC   Aye, here he's, here he's, here he's.

Doctor Broon

    Here comes in old Doctor Broon,

    The best old doctor in the toon.

And the MC says,

    And what can you cure, Doctor?

Doctor Broon

    I can cure all sorts.

MC   And what kind o all sorts.

Doctor Broon

    Liquorice allsorts. I've got a little bottle here of inksy pinksy parleyvous, all covered

> over wi cats' feathers and midges' ribs.
> I shall put a little to his nose.

And he puts it to his toes.

> I shall put a little to his toes.

And he puts it to his nose.

> Rise up Jack and sing a song.

King George Once I was dead and now I'm alive.
God bless the doctor that made me survive.

The other fellow that comes in is old Beelzebub. ...

Beelzebub Oh here am I, old Beelzebub
And over my shoulder I carry a club
And in ma hands a frying pan.
I think myself a jolly old man. ...

And then here's the yin. This is Johnny Funny and he's usually dressed wi an old tile hat on and he usually feenishes it off. He says:

Johnny Funny

> Here am I wee Johnny Funny,
> I'm the yin that collects the money.
> Lang, lang pooches doon tae my knees,
> Yin for pennies, and yin for bawbees.

That's about all. ...

BL 'Ladies and gentlemen, you'll never grow fat ...'
PT 'If you dinnae put a penny in the old man's hat.' That's right!
BL Noo did you sing that 'Once I was dead and now I'm alive'?
PT Yes.
BL What did you sing it to? ...
PT

Once I was dead ...

Oh, I canna mind.

BL

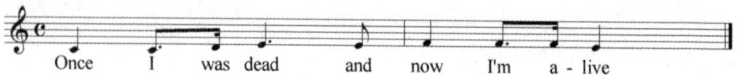

Once I was dead and now I'm a-live

PT That's right. ...

BL It's a polka tune but I don't know the right name. And did you sing 'We'll all join hands'?

PT No, we didnae do that. ... As I say, we had the Moor, that would be what you called Turkish Knight, an he was aye blackened, ken, and then ... we whiles had a singer singing a song like 'The Bonnie Wells o Wearie' or somethin like that. You aye gied a wee bit extra, ye ken. ... It wis more or less impromptu depending on how many you had and hoo many wis there, you see. ... As I say, the last man that ever I minded was Wee Johnny Funny. And he aye had a tile hat or a bowler hat or some kind o hat like that, but it was usually a tile, if you could get it.

EL And he collected in it?

PT And he went roon and collected wi it. Well, say the likes o, we'll say Murray o Spittal, maybe Murray would ... invite us and maybe have half a dozen other farmers in, ye ken. ... And then there was Latto Morrison, ken, and then Elsie, she would come through, ken, that was the maid then. An Elsie wad come through and there was the big front room you did it up in Latto Morrison's. The same wi the one at Spittal. It was the big room that looked doon ontae the water that you did it in. Aye, we were aye invited intae the big –

BL Say an ordinary house, the like o, you know, just a wee house in the street, did you just do it in ...

PT Usually the man, you ken, the same as I am the noo, you ken, the man sittin on the wan side o the fire and the mother was sitting on the other and there they – and the bairns – and there they were and you got a tanner.

EL I was just going to say about how much would you get?

PT	About sixpence maybe, maybe thruppence sometimes.
EL	What about the big houses, how much?
PT	Oh, I've seen us getting as much as a pound.
EL	Yes. You were really out for money and you gave the money in?
PT	The money was given to a man called, well in my particular day it was a man called Cocky Moore –
BL	That's Bobby Moore.
PT	Bobby Moore. And wee Bobby. … well, he actually kept the money and, as I say, roughly after everything was sort of paid, the coal and that, he started dividin. And you see as you went each evening to go out and collect the wood you had a wee book and your name was in the wee book, for every night you were out you got a tick. Say you had ten ticks for ten evenings, well you got so much for each, maybe thruppence for each evening you'd been oot if it was available.
EL	So you'd get it for going out siguising, would you?
PT	As well as collecting.
EL	Yes.
PT	As well as the collecting. I've seen me get – the most I ever got in my life was seven and six. But that gave me a good day in Glasgow at the – what do you call it, ken, where the fair, the circus is held? – the Kelvin Hall.
BL	Kelvin Hall, yes.
PT	We looked forward to the Kelvin Hall in Glasgow. We were able to get a day oot in Glasgow.
EL	Where did you check in to get your name –
PT	Oh! Mr Moore's every night.
EL	Where did he live? …
PT	He stayed in a house in the square.
EL	So, did you get all dressed up to go and see him and check in? Was that –
PT	No, no, you actually –
BL	He'd know by your black face.
PT	Oh well, most o the time my mother and father did not

	object to us doing wir paraphernalia, but there was quite a number o mothers that did. And as I say, we carried the candle with us and the corks and then –
BL	Did you say something about you goin to bed once without washing your face?
PT	Oh, aye by jings! Did I not get a lundering for that! I think Alan and I were both employed at that night. See Alan – actually he wasn't that much older than me – he was still guising, siguising when I was still –
EL	Were you in the same group together?
PT	Aye, oh aye. You never broke – there weren't two groups. There was always only the one group. There might be ten of us and it might only be five, you see.
BL	But there werenae different groups going round.
PT	Oh, no, not in the top of the town, no, no, no, no.
BL	The Westrow ones would be a different group?
PT	Aye, well, they were a different area of town. That was the only time there was rivalry. Really, rivalry was that particular time with the bonfire.
EL	So there was only one group for the top of the town?
PT	Yes, oh yes.
EL	And so you'd all be quite keen to get into it?
PT	Oh aye, aye. Oh, I think on some nights, of course, you ken the usual style, 'No, you're too wee' sort of style.
BL	Did you ever have girls in it?
PT	No, we never had a girl in it.
BL	See, Lizzie Broon wis in it, she told me.
PT	That could be, but I've never –
BL	Do you mind the Cranstons in Kirk Style?
PT	Yes.
BL	Well, I'd an aunt married, you know, one of the Cranstons married my uncle. She said, she maintains she did it.
PT	Yes, that could be. … The persons that done it wi me would be Sandy Robertson, Sandy Whitefold, ah, John Whitefield, Wilson Arroll, ken, we were all about ages. There werenae a

great deal o difference between us. ... But funny enough, you know, you thought nothing about walking away to Heavieside and Spittal and these bits, you know. And you used to carry yon – have you ever seen them, the little? – We bought candles from the Jenny MacMath's, but the wee holders came fae your faither's shop, just like wee torches but they had wee candles sitting inside.

BL   Kind of like a jelly jar kind of thing?

PT   No, but they were metal, ken, they got awfie hot in the top. We used tae hing them on sticks.

BL   Aye, just like a wee lantern.

PT   Just like a wee lantern. And your father sold them. I think they were only tuppence or thruppence. But the only thing is ken, as I say, they got very hot at the top because they were kind o serrated, ribbed, you know what I mean. They werena very big. And, of course in a windy night the candle blew out because there was no glass in them or anything, there were little apertures on it if you understand. You could still see with them like. But that's the sort o thing that we took.

EL   So as to show your way up –

PT   Aye, certain places. But, funny enough, your eyes got used to the dark when you were born in the country. I don't know, even yet I've got quite good eyesight in the dark. ... My eyes just seemed to get accustomed to the dark. ... I would start about ten and would maybe do it for three years, three and a half, because I started work as a young painter's apprentice. An of course you give these things up and start looking for girls, you know. You get out of these things. ... I think it was all the same ages, roughly from about ten to thirteen. Just about, that would be the ages. You might get an odd one about fourteen or that but very very rarely.

EL   Once you'd set up the group for the year, did you go always out together then for the rest of that session or did some people drop out and others come in?

PT   Well, some people sometimes dropped out and you got others came in, but more or less, say, you started away – it was usually about collecting the wood. There would be, say, about ten of us, and that ten would do the actual collecting the wood. Now, it was a sort o understanding after that if you collected the wood you got siguising, so comin or goin one or two fell out. They would only fall out for a night. You know, maybe no come on a Monday. You see you went out every night o the week for a whole fortnight, every night, except Sundays, of course. You didn't go out on a Sunday, oh, no, no.

EL   What about Christmas? Was it –

PT   No, nothing like that. No, no, no. There was nothing about that at Christmas. In fact I never got my presents at Christmas. I always got my presents at New Year.

EL   Did you go out on Christmas evening?

PT   No, nothing like that, no. Oh, if we went out it was not because it was Christmas. We went out because it was for the benefit of the fire, if you understand what I'm trying to say? You didn't go out because it was particularly Christmas time you –

EL   It didn't stop you going out?

PT   No, no, no, no. It didn't stop us, no, no. But I mean you didn't go out because – you would nowadays, you know how they go out carol-singin and all that. In that particular day there were nothing like that in Biggar.

EL   It was just a kind of lead-up to the New Year?

PT   Correct. The New Year was the main happy event, as far as we were concerned anyway. ...

EL   How did the Doctor carry his bottle?

PT   Oh it was always a proper big Gladstone bag, the bigger the better. And the mouldier, the mouldier, or whatever you like to caa it, and the dirtier it wis the better and it was always, you ken, a great big bottle too, you know.

BL   A big bottle.

PT	It was aye a big bottle and it was usually dirty green water or something.
BL	Oh, you had something in it.
PT	Oh, you aye had something in it. And whiles you forgot yourself if you didnae like the fellow, you ken; you took the cork oot! But it was always filled. I mean, it was always something in it. And you had bits of bones. You'd pick out bones and, you ken, a pair o pliers and a bit of saw. You always had a saw, ye ken.
EL	What did you do with it?
PT	Just laid these aside, ye see, until you got tae this great big bottle. And then you picked this bottle up and he put it down to his toes – that was his nose, of course, and his nose was his toes. An you got some antics.
EL	And what did you all say when he came in? Did you all speak together or not?
PT	No, you had an MC. That was the fellow that went in and shouted 'A room, a room' and he went in an he kind o opened the doors and he walked in. And he was usually dressed very flamboyantly, ken. He usually had a fancy – if you could get yin of yon, what I'd call Napoleonic hats, type of thing. Sometimes you'd just paper hats.
BL	What about a kilt?
PT	Aye. They wore kilts tae, aye, och, onything went, anything – jackets outside-in went.
BL	Who said 'Here is he'? Who said that? Was that just Doctor Brown that said that?
PT	Aye. No. 'Here he is, here he is, here comes in old Doctor Brown', that was the MC.
BL	Everybody didnae say that?
PT	Oh, no, no, no, no.
BL	See, that's different frae what I heard.
PT	But actually your dress could be onything. I mean, I'll take your master o ceremonies. He usually had an old set of tails, ye ken. And he'd have a fancy waistcoat that usually –

probably made that hisself, probably a big old waistcoat that he got from somebody, yon old fancy checked yins, and big troosers that was much too big for him and a wooden sword. And then George, well you just made a cardboard crown for him, you ken, and that kind o thing. An you got coloured troosers, you ken, if you could get them. I remember once I got an old pair o pyjamas, ken, and put them ower mine. Well, of course, we wore shorts, as you know boys wore shorts. ... And then Doctor Broon well, as I said, he usually had spats if you could get them. Or, and I'll tell you another thing that a lot of them sometimes wore, was thon – what did you call them? – gaiters, what you call them, leggings, ken. You got mind you used to get them fancy buttons ones. Ah well, we used to wear aa they kind o things, onything. In fact, you wore anything. ... [Trimmings] were only an added attraction. You tied them onto different bits o sticks and this kind o thing. You made yourself, you know. Maybe you had a hat, you'd get a lot o old trimmins and pin them onto the hat.

BL   Wallpaper trimmings?

PT   Aye, aye, so they cascaded doon, ye ken. This, see, Johnny Funny, if I remember rightly, I'll tell ye, it was a bunnet, an army bunnet. It wis a bunnet, a richt blanket bunnet, you know, the old kind of old fashioned blanket bunnets? An I think it was wee Bobby Michael that did Johnny Funny and that was what he was wearing, you ken, this bunnet.

BL   So it wasn't necessarily a tile hat?

PT   No, no, no, no. Oh, you'd wear onything. The only yins that we tried [to get] was tile hats for master o ceremonies and Doctor Brown and that. Ye tried to get straight troosers and all this kind o – a walking stick. See, as I say, in his bag he had a pair of pliers, a hammer, a saw, ye ken, onything, a bone, ye ken it was usually a muckle big ham bone, you know, to make it look more ridiculous. But it was funny. A lot o the funnier things that we did in they days were really daft things. I mean you didnae stick to what you would call the paperwork because you didn't carry on this way. And an awful lot of cases and you'd be doing a big house, say the likes o Bing Anderson's hoose, and he says 'That's no right'. This is, see, he knew it. And he said, see, 'I didnae do that', you see. ...

EL   What would you do then? Would you change it?

PT   We would change it for *him*. So long as you got money.

EL   Did you ever remember one of these particular points when anyone would tell you that was wrong or right?

PT   Oh, I think we would be told that we were wrong in just about every old house we went intae. Old Thomson and them all, just about everyone. 'Oh, I never did that when I was a laddie', you see. But then, you see, by the same token I've forgotten half o it. I mean that's only really what I can remember. ...

EL   And did these older people feel that you ought to be doing it the way they had done it?

PT   Oh, yes, oh aye. ...

BL   It was just maybe one word! 'But that wasnae right.'

PT   You could see them sitting. I mind o old Thomson sitting wi the pipe and he's sitting listening, see, an then you was only getting tuppence! And then he'd tell ye, 'Ah! but you missed that oot', or 'You missed this oot'. ... But you see, some houses you went to they wanted a kind o concert. This is what they wanted.

BL   For tuppence!

PT   For tuppence. ... It was always tradition, money. ... As I say an old dear wad gie ye a couple o apples, but you thought nothing about it, and she might put a penny in which was quite acceptable. But by and large I would say the average from the ordinary folk was thruppence.

BL   And that was for the coal?

PT   Aye, oh aye. Well, there was always a ton o coal bought, always. ... And there was always ... five gallon o paraffin

	bought, always a five-gallon drum, and it was delivered there and the coal was delivered wi Johnny Uppence and Jimmy Uppence and then there was the tar was bought at that time, … maybe about five gallon o tar, maybe about ten gallon o tar.
EL	Well, this about the wallpaper trimmings, they were cascading from the hat?
PT	Well, not necessarily from the hat. You could have them wi your stick, anyone that carried a stick.
EL	Who would? Who would be carrying a stick?
PT	Oh well, Doctor Brown for one and nearly aa the rest would have them. Och, we would have used them for everything. You tied them round your body and everything.
EL	Did you tie them round your waist?
PT	Aye, ontae the belts wi a bit o string, tucked them into the string.
EL	And what did they do? Kind o dangle down?
PT	Aye, dangle down, onything to look daft. But it was mainly the hats they put them.
EL	You seem to have been carrying a lot of things because you were travelling –
PT	No, not really.
EL	Did you have these sticks with the light at the end of it?
PT	Aye, well that was only when we were going out to the country we had sticks. … There was something else that we used to use and I'm trying to think whit it was.
EL	For what?
PT	For decoration.
BL	Inside-oot jackets.
PT	Oh, that was a kind o foregone conclusion.
BL	What else is kind o useful that's for throwing away?
PT	I think it was some o the leather trimmings that we got off Bobby Smith, aye, fer putting them on wir swords, an that kind a thing, ken, tying the leather. …

EL   Did you keep any of the costume from one year to the next?

PT   No, not really, no. Your costumes was more or less – well I'm talking about my day more or less well, not stolen, filched! You wad even take them off a scarecrow. I remember once in particular, we were going out by Heavieside an there was an old tile hat on a scarecrow. Jist as you go doon the brae, ye ken, after you leave Heavieside you make for Spittal, ken. It was part o Heavieside field. Here's this scarecrow an it had a battered tile hat that was better than yin we had, so we took it! ... Bobby Smith was a great man for gieing things, old jackets and, ye ken, the tails, the old tails and that.

EL   What was he? Was he the leather worker?

PT   Aye.

BL   The saddler. ...

EL   How far did you walk when you went out on this –

PT   Oh, I would say farthest would be, what? – Skirling, three and a half mile, Coulter four, about four mile.

EL   How many houses could you get in in an evening?

PT   Oh well, you were very fortunate in the like of these large houses you'd be fortunate if you got five in.

EL   When would you start?

PT   Oh, seven o'clock. You were out by seven o'clock. You did Latto Morrison's; you did Blackwood; you did Heavieside – that was three – doon intae Spittal – that was four, come back roon. If you were lucky, you went ower tae Skirling Mill Farm, ken, an –

BL   Skirling Hoose.

PT   No.

BL   Did you ever do Skirling Hoose?

PT   Aye, but you did that another night.

BL   Were the Carmichaels there?

PT   Yes, aye, aye. The Carmichaels were there. ... We went in the wee lodge gate. The actual wee gate at the side. You didnae go roond to the front, what I call the front in there lookin into the square. ... Went in that wee gate and you went through intae the garden. ...

EL So was your route pretty set? I mean, could you do it on a map, that you went here this evening then you went there the next evening? Did you have a sort of routine at all?

PT No, no really. It was just a case o how you felt that particular nicht, would we walk to Skirling.

EL It would be the weather partly, I suppose?

PT Well, the weather governed a lot o the far-out ones I would say, the like o Skirling an that, you picked a good evening for that.

EL Yes, so you would do the ones more in town –

PT Oh, aye, the like o say the like o half-wet nights. And some nights you never did it at all.

EL And you'd just remember what houses and what you'd done?

PT That's right. It came sort o natural to you because nearly every boy was a message boy including myself, and therefore you knew every house and every person and who stayed there, and in fact what you were likely to get there, what reception you got. You know, you had it all weighed up in your mind.

EL Did you ever get refused?

PT Yes, we did, but very, very rarely, I must admit. I'm not going to mention the names who refused us, but I could. ... But it was really peculiar, they just couldnae be bothered wi ye you know and they were Biggeronians who's been here all their days. ...

EL So what happened in a position, a situation like that? What would happen when you went?

PT Oh, you jist walked away. But you got your own back. You played peenytick or break-the-glass or something like –

BL It didnae pay them tae refuse!

PT You know what peenytick is?

EL Tell me!

PT Well, peenytick, you get a big old-fashioned safety pin – one of these right old-fashioned safety pins – and ye stick it in the window about maybe eighteen inches up from the sash, you see, stick it in and you thread your thread through it wi a big heavy button or a washer on it. And you're across the other side o the road, you see, pullin this, and this is going back and forrit and it's ticking on the windae. It's going tick! every time you pull it, it's gaain tick, tick, you see. And we called it pinnytick because every time you pulled this – and of course they would go out and they cannae see. I mean, it's very difficult tae see especially if you done it the proper way. And the other one was you'd knock at their door an you'd an old bottle an you'd knock at the door and break the bottle an tap at the window and they'd come out shouting thinking you had broke their windows.

EL Would you do that on the evenings you'd been refused, on the same evening?
PT Ah, not necessarily, but –
BL All the year round.
PT Aye. ... I remember once guising and I was Beelzebub and this is true. The man's livin today I believe. An he dressed as a ghost. And he's going 'Who-o-o-' you see. An I hit him wi the club! So he didnae do the ghost for a while!
EL What was he –
PT He was trying to frighten us, aye, he was trying to frighten us when we were going out guising or siguising.
EL Was this out in the country somewhere?
PT Aye, aye. In fact this was the country then, up here.
EL What was the group of boys called, do you know?
PT We hadn't any names.
BL The siguisers.
PT Just the siguisers, that's all.
EL So if you saw the Westrow lot would you just say 'There's the Westrow'?
PT Aye, 'There's the Westraw'.
EL Yes.

PT Aye, no, you didnae have any – No, actually, we didnae really fight that awfie often, ye ken, kind of rivalry. It wisnae, there there was no blood and thunder really in it. An I mean, there was no knives or anything like that. It was mainly fists and that, you know. I mean, it wis only – I don't think we ever had a real fight in the true sense – no like they have nowadays.

EL Would you say 'This is our part?'

PT Oh, I mean, the borderline was there. It wasn't actually defined in the sense o a map. But you know that was the border line. You could go up the length o the two churches. But you couldn't go down the Burnbraes. You see, you could walk up tae the Manse and come doon what they call Norcrofts. ... You could go doon that a way but you couldnae go down the Westrow, go down the burn. Aye, oh aye, that was you feenished, sort o style.

EL Just explain to me a wee bit how you got your names ticked off? I mean, how did this happen in the early part of the evening?

PT For taking the parts like?

EL Yes.

PT Yes, yes. Well, as I say, they usually picked a – well Sandy Robertson saw nights for taking charge. And he'd say, 'Right, you, you're Johnny Funny; you're Beelzebub; you're Sir William Wallace; you're –', see everybody got their part. An everybody could take – funny enough, everybody could take every part, you see. That particular time I don't think there'd be any more than five of us. The average was about five, maybe six at the very most.

EL And where did this happen?

PT Met at the bonfire or at that Cocky Moore's hoose or outside his house. And you just sort of automatically – it depended. You usually left at about seven o'clock in the evening – slightly after it sometimes – maybe. And it was just an automatic, 'Well, we're going to Skirling tonight'.

Fig. 1

The fight (*The Scots Magazine*, December 1956, 197–201).

(*Copyright:* D. C. Thomson & Co. Ltd)

Fig. 2

The bargaining for the cure (*The Scots Magazine*, December 1956, 197–201).

(*Copyright:* D. C. Thomson & Co. Ltd)

Fig. 3

Singing the blessing (*The Scots Magazine*, December 1956, 197–201).

(*Copyright:* D. C. Thomson & Co. Ltd)

Fig. 4

Setting off to the next house (*The Scots Magazine*, December 1956, 197–201).

(*Copyright:* D. C. Thomson & Co. Ltd)

Fig. 5 Wat Ramage.
(*Source:* School of Scottish Studies Archive)

Fig. 6 Andrew Rennie.
(*Source:* School of Scottish Studies Archive)

Fig. 7 William Brown.
(*Source:* School of Scottish Studies Archive)

Figs 8–18
An outdoor performance at Biggar of a version with ten characters produced by Brian Lambie in 1982. Fig. 8 character is called Room (played by Diane Ritchie)

(*Source:* Emily Lyle, School of Scottish Studies Archive)

FIGS 9–12
Wee Yin (Lorna Clark)
King George (David Hodgson)
Turkey Snipe (Colin Moore)
Beelzebub (Graham Gordon)
(*Source*: Emily Lyle, School of Scottish Studies Archive)

FIGS 13–16

Galashians
(John Tweedie)

Tea, Toast and Butter
(Felicity Gerraghty)

Sir William Wallace
(Steven Bolton)

Doctor Brown
(Michelle Gillespie)

FIG. 17
(opposite page, top left)

Johnnie Funny
(Jacqueline Tweedie)

(*Source:* Emily Lyle, School of Scottish Studies Archive)

FIG. 18
King George and Galashians fight.

FIG. 19
Room announces 'Here's two warriors come to fight' as Sir William Wallace and King George prepare for battle.

FIG. 20
Doctor Brown cures King George while Sir William Wallace looks on.

(*Source:* Emily Lyle, School of Scottish Studies Archive)

Stills from a video of Andrew Rennie performing the play.

FIG. 21: 'The first young man that I call in/Is the Admiral stout and bold.'

22: 'Here comes in the Admiral,/The Admiral stout and bold.'

23: 'Take out yer sword and try, sir.'

24: 'Here's two warriors going to fight/That never fought before.'

(opposite page)

25: 'Here comes in old Doctor Brown,/The best old doctor in the town.'

26: 'I've a little bottle in my waistcoat pocket.'

27: 'A drop on the nose, a drop on the chin.'

28: 'Once I was dead but now I'm alive.'

29: 'And all the little babies around the table too.'

30: 'We wish you all a good Hogmanay and a happy New Year.'

31: 'If ye've anything to spare,/Jist pop it in there.'

(Images 21–31: *Source:* School of Scottish Studies Archive)

Five boys from Kippen perform the play as taught them by Andrew Rennie.

FIG. 32: The Admiral (Cameron Sharp) and Galoshins (Thomas Cassidy) fight, encouraged by Keep Silence (Craig MacDonnell).

33: Doctor Brown (Tommy Smith) enters.

34: Keekem Funny (Alan Edmiston) prepares to take the collection.

(*Source:* School of Scottish Studies Archive)

	And each man was given his part and sometimes you were given two parts, so what you did you went out and you just changed jackets or something and this sort of thing. You just came back in, I mean.
EL	Would the Doctor wait outside?
PT	Aye, he was one of the last, aye. You always had to have a good man for the Doctor and a good man for the MC. The man that was the MC – of course he'd to stand the brunt o any trouble that was comin cos, I mean, doors weren't locked. You must remember that doors weren't locked in these days, or maybe a back door or that – front doors were very, very rarely locked.
BL	Nobody set the dog on you?
PT	Aye, I've had that, and you could run, I tell ye, you could run! ...
EL	You were saying that you were usually the one that knocked.
PT	Well, usually. I quite often took Doctor Brown's part.
EL	Oh, you did?
PT	Aye, and sometimes I took the MC but, when you took the MC, you always knocked. You had to go to the door first.
EL	What sort of trouble did you meet?
PT	Very little actually, I'll be honest wi you. ...
EL	Did you feel you had to knock at the doors even if you –
PT	Well, you just knocked. Well, actually, what you did was bang, bang, opened the door and shouted, 'A room, a room'. And if he didn't, you got 'A room, a room' back. They just got a grip of you and lightly pushed you back out and that was that, you just – There were no arguments or anything. But they very rarely done that because they knew they would get the worst o it before the year was finished, you know, because you sort of ganged up on them and –
BL	Kind of insurance to let you do it.
PT	Well, for thruppence it was a very safe. When you think o it, I mean you really did gie them a rough time o it throughout the year, ken, if anyone did onything like that to you. ...

BL   Did you ever put a divot in anybody's chimney.

PT   Yes, as a matter o fact, I was just talkin about that the other night. I remember ... the wee corner shop an ... it was an old codger that was in the next place and he was always getting onto us boys. And I remember we climbed, went through Boa's Close, up onto his paraffin shed, fae his paraffin shed onto where old Mrs MacDougall stayed, and fae there ontae the other roof. An I was on one roof – I cannae mind whae was on the other yin, it would maybe be big Tam Gibson, but it'll no maitter – an somebody's on the other yin, and we threw the sod to each ither, we just drapped it on his chimney an then went across the road. And the next thing is the old fire engine was oot. The two Grahams, and I cannae mind o who the other two were, were trying to put it oot.

EL   Was this just sheer mischief?

PT   Just sheer bad mischief!

EL   Did you have anything against him?

PT   Ah well, he was always picking on us poor laddies, ye ken.

7   *Mrs Sheila Duffy* (née *Harris*) – *Muirkirk, 1933–1934*

I recorded this conversation (SA2001.025) on 26 February 2001 in an Honours Theory and Methods class in Scottish Ethnology at the School of Scottish Studies, University of Edinburgh. Participants were class members Kirsten Anderson, Angela McCulloch, Andrew Morrison and Emma Vickerstaff and a visiting scholar, Terry Gunnell. Sheila Duffy had been reminded of the play when she had seen the video 'Keep Silence and Company: The Kippen *Galoshins*' in a previous Ethnology course. She had written out the text she remembered and those present took the various parts and then entered into discussion. The text here is as spoken by Mrs Duffy herself at a later point in the recording. The descriptions of the action are as she wrote them out.

> Guisers enter the kitchen. A girl, Bessie, sweeps the floor with a besom, singing or humming, then goes out.

All	Stir up the fire and gie us a light
	For in this hoose there's going to be a fight.
	If you don't believe the words I say
	Call in Saint George to clear the way.
St George	I am St George and from England sprung,
	Many deeds of wonder I have done.
	Oft times a dragon almost struck me dead,
	But I drew my trusty sword and cut off his head.
	I travelled the world all round and round
	And a man to equal me I never found.
All	Call in Sir William Wallace.
Wallace	Here comes I Sir William Wallace
	Underneath disguise.
	I have both sword and shield
	To meet my enemies in the battlefield.
All	Call in King Robert the Bruce.
Bruce	I am King Robert the Bruce,
	Battle axe over my shoulder.
	Now I'm in my native land
	I'm feeling very bold.
Beelzebub	Here comes I old Beelzebub,
	Over my shoulder I carry a club,
	In my hand a dripping pan,
	I count myself a jolly old man.
	It's money I want and money I crave.
	If I don't get money I'll sweep you to your grave.

Keekum Funny	
	Here comes I Wee Keekum Funny,
	I'm the man who takes the money.
	Great big pooches doon to ma knees,
	Fine for haudin wee bawbees.
All	Call in Gloshins
Gloshins	I am a gallant soldier
	And Gloshins is my name,
	With sword and buckler by my side
	I hope to win the game.
St George	The game sir, the game sir,
	'Tis not within your power.
	I could cut you up in pieces
	In less than half an hour.
Gloshins	Nay.
St George	What's that you say!
Gloshins	Take out your purse and pay.
St George	I have no purse to pay.
Gloshins	Then draw your sword and prepare for a fight.

They fight. Gloshins falls dead.

St George	A doctor, a doctor, five pounds for a doctor.
Doctor Broon	
	Here am I old Doctor Broon,
	The best old doctor in the toon.
St George	What can you cure?
Dr Broon	All sorts.
St George	What's all sorts?
Dr Broon	If there were nineteen deevils in one man's heid,
	I could knock twenty of them off.
St George	Is that all, sir? Can you cure deid men?
Dr Broon	Yes, sir, I have a bottle of inky-pinky in my waistcoat pocket.
	Put a little on his back, put a little on his heid.
	Rise up Jack and sing a song.

| *All* | Once we were deid but now we're alive |
| | Thanks to the doctor who made us revive. |

Each player sings one song while Keekum Funny goes round collecting money and food.

SD Well, that's what I remember sixty-seven years ago in East Ayrshire in a place called Muirkirk and it was every Halloween and the boys used to go round the big houses. This was a farm – a big farm kitchen – and the headmaster's house and another farmer's house and a big lodge – about five big houses. And they didn't rehearse it or anything, but I think Bessie – she didn't appear again, she only came in at the beginning – and I think she probably helped them. And their clothes were old jackets turned inside out, but the Doctor had a top hat, I remember that, and a black coat, and they all had their faces blacked with cork, and then at the end … [they] got … halfpennies and pennies – this was about 1933 – and lots of apples, oranges, nuts and lots of sweeties. …

KA What sort of age were the boys?

SD They would be about nine or ten and, as I said, Bessie was probably about twelve. She was probably somebody's big sister. Yeah, nine or ten, and I was about seven or eight.

EV What songs would they sing afterwards?

SD Oh yes, just the usual songs at the time. I was trying to remember. One was 'Old Faithful' – does anybody know that? – a western one, yes, all the children sang it: 'Old Faithful, we'll roam the range together', oh, it was lovely, and then 'Red Sails in the Sunset', I can remember and – there were several songs which were popular songs at the time. …

AM How important was the money and food that they got given?

SD Very important. Those children were poor. It was the Depression in a mining village. … They got very little money … pennies, but yes, oh they enjoyed the apples and the oranges and the nuts and the sweets and they got plenty by the time they had been round the five houses and the Keekum Funny had the big kind of sugar bags, he had big trousers and he had sugar bags and everything was put in. ...The families they went to were the big houses – the farms, the farming area – the children, apart from their being miners' children, they were farm-labourers' children, they were all poor and so I mean it was a big thing. There was certainly no question of their mothers not wanting them to go. And there was no danger, they could just wander around in gangs.

KA Can you remember if they had any particular actions, like on the video we saw the arms swinging.

SD Oh yes, they did that, and of course the fight. ... They had wooden swords and St George, I can remember he had a shield ... he had a white cloak with a big red cross on it. ... The doctor I can remember vividly with his top hat and Gloshins and Keekum Funny. He was a little boy, a funny little boy anyway, quite a little comic – of course I knew them all at school – so he must have wanted to be Keekum Funny. ...

KA Was there one part which everybody wanted to play?

SD I don't think so, no, or they might have played another year, played another part. Everybody knew all the words and I had totally forgotten the words until I started doing this and it all gradually came back from the recesses of my brain. ... I can now remember, you know, the big kitchen and oh it was a very happy occasion, a warm kitchen, you know, a big fire, and then afterwards we all had a party, you know, something to eat, and it was all very happy. So the guisers were really – people looked forward to them and I don't remember any question about people, grown-ups, going on about begging or anything like that. They didn't think of it as begging, and the children just enjoyed it.

EL You said they were mostly boys?

SD Mostly boys, just that one girl, but in the audience there were girls but they didn't take part.

EL	Tell us a little more about the girl. What did she do exactly? …
SD	Bessie, oh, as I say she was bigger. She was a big girl. She had on probably her mother or her granny's pinny – you know those pinnies they used to wear – and something over her head. And she didn't do anything else. She just came in with a besom – you know what a besom is? a kind of broom – and she just swept all round kind of clearing the area and then she went out again, so I rather think that she – cos they would probably need a bit of help all these little boys, so she probably helped them.
KA	Was there a particular song that she sang? …
SD	I think she was just humming. No, I can't remember her actually singing any song. …
EL	Was there any bit of the play sung?
SD	Oh, they sang it all.
EL	They sang it all? …
SD	Oh, yes, they sang it all in a sort of a way. …
EL	You've begun to give us quite a picture of how they were dressed up. So, you've seen that the Bessie with the pinafore –
SD	Yes, a pinny, and the boys had jackets turned inside out and their fathers' shirts and the jackets were their fathers' jackets too and … of course they had blacked faces or else they had masks, false faces, and we never really knew who they were. … Some people might have known who they were but they didn't take their masks off or anything. They went away again and we didn't know who they were. … What else did they wear? Keekum Funny of course wore the big trousers. … The thing is they were all old clothes, I mean they were just … the top hat, the doctor, and he had a frock coat, a black frock coat, which he must have got from somewhere, and a top hat.
EL	And where did he carry his medicine? …
SD	He might have had a bag, I can't remember. I know he got out this inkypinky, whatever it was, it was in a bottle and

	he got it out and he put it on Gloshins' back. …
TG	Now did people take the same part each year?
SD	Well, I can't remember. I don't think so cos each year they would be a year older, wouldn't they, so I suppose as they got too old they would stop doing it and the younger ones would come up, so I think probably each year would be different boys. …
TG	And no particular organiser within the group? …
SD	Well I didn't know that, but thinking of it I think the girl cos she was definitely – she was a big girl, she was twelve and she was a big girl so I should think that she kind've was looking after them. Some of the little boys were only seven or eight. But I can remember – once you start remembering – I can remember it very vividly.
EL	You can see it, you can picture it?
SD	Absolutely. I enjoyed it.
TG	The houses that were visited … was there a particular route that they took?
SD	Yes, they lived in the village in the miners' cottages and then we were all about three miles out, so there was a big farm and there was the big house and then a bit further on there was another big farm and then down in the village itself were one or two houses, but just particular houses. Oh yes, there was the manager of the Coal Board, he had a big house so they always went there. …
EL	Would you feel like actually naming the various houses? … The order they went round in?
SD	Well, right. There was the farm, Old House Burn Farm – that's where I saw it in the kitchen of that – and then next door was where we lived, it was called Old House Burn, and then there was Cross Flat, that was the next over field, Cross Flat and the Clarks, and then another big farm, the McCallums', sort of across the main road, and then down near the pit was the manager's house, they probably ended up there. …

KA Were those parts where everyone speaks, would the audience be encouraged to –

SD No, no, it was just the players.

EL You're actually envisaging, you can remember this, so if you were in, you know, you were in the room, can you just describe what happens when it begins?

SD Oh right. Well we were all sitting in the kitchen, and we knew that the guisers were coming, so we all sat in the kitchen round a big fire – I can remember the fire and lots of chairs and settees and so on, quite a lot of people, and then, as I say, they came in. I think they said something like, 'Here come the guisers' or something like that. They didn't knock, they just came in. 'Oh, here they come.' And then the Bessie came in and in a way cleared a space. But it was all waiting, everything was ready waiting for them, and then they just began. …

AMcC Was this on Halloween night?

SD Halloween night, yes. …

EL I'm sure you're assuming this was after dark?

SD Oh, it was. It was dark.

EL And I'm just trying to imagine this Bessie, what exactly she did when she came – What did she – They came in together. Did they come in as a group?

SD No, no, they didn't, she came in first. … That's right, they all stayed outside the door and they probably said, 'Here come the guisers', and they all waited at the door and she came in … and she just, with the besom just swept everything and went out again. Kind of strange. …

EL So when you said she was humming – I don't want to put ideas into your head but would that be the tune that they were going to be using?

SD No, it could have been anything. She might have been humming, you know, 'My Bonnie Lies Over the Ocean' or something, just anything. She would just, she'd know she'd

	have to hum just while she'd be sweeping, she'd be humming.
EL	You're making quite distinct sweeping movements there.
SD	Oh yes, the sweeping was very distinct.
EL	And describe the besom, what's it like?
SD	Well, it's a broom with a broom handle but what's at the end? Bristles, I think, bristles all tied round. I think it was used for sweeping leaves. And she just did this kind of almost ritual sweeping cos it didn't need to be swept, it was perfectly clean, but it was just as if she was clearing a space.
AM	And was the besom, was that something which was used in daily life?
SD	Yes, yes.
AM	It wasn't made specially for this occasion?
SD	No, no. They'd borrowed it from home. Everybody had one. … After they had all their goodies, then they left to go to the next house and we would all just have something to eat too, and just chat about it. …
KA	Would you talk amongst yourselves afterwards about who you thought each of the guisers were?
SD	Yes, yes, we did try to find out who but we never knew, well, I didn't, perhaps the grown-ups did, but the boys were very particular that we shouldn't recognise them.
AM	Did they disguise their voices?
SD	Well, they put on funny voices, yes.
AM	So that they wouldn't be recognised?
SD	Yes. …
TG	Masks, could they be bought in the village shop?
SD	Yes, yes. They didn't even call them masks, they called them false faces. …
TG	And what sort of faces on them?
SD	Oh, horrible faces, you know, gargoyles and things, monsters.
TG	Beelzebub didn't go out of his way to make himself frightening?

SD	No, he didn't. I never even thought he was frightening, but I know he was dressed in black. ...
EL	[After Mrs Duffy spoke the words of the play.] They changed voices? They kind of put on –
SD	They put on funny voices, yes, some were squeaky voices.

8 David Laurie and Mrs Margaret Muir (née *Laurie*) – Kirkcowan, 1921–1925

Mrs Muir made contact with me in response to the *Scots Magazine* appeal of January 1982 and arranged for me to meet with her and her brother, David, at her home in Glasgow to talk over the Halloween play and their other memories of life in Kirkcowan (SA1982.115, 116, 117). Mrs Muir was surprised to find her brother using the word 'clog' in the Beelzebub speech; she had always thought the word spoken was 'club'. David Laurie performed in one form of the play in Kirkcowan and later performed in another form of it in the town of Newton Stewart, seven miles from Kirkcowan [9].

MM	I've asked around just in conversation on the off-chance that anybody else had known one or other version of it. ...
EL	So you really have tried and no one has known it?
MM	No, no. The only pertinent answer I got was saying to a friend who was born in Dumbarton, my own age, 'What did you call guisers when you were a little girl?', and without hesitation she said, 'Galoshins'.
DL	That name never came into our vocabulary at all.
MM	Neither did guisers.
DL	No.
MM	They were just the Black Boys. ... Well, I can remember as a mere female knowing that the boys and their friends were in

a shed of ours with the bits of wood and the scout knife type of things –

DL   Making swords.

MM   They weren't kept from year to year, they were reconstructed each time. What I don't know is whether you did any rehearsal of the actual speech ... Or whether it was just in everybody's bones –

DL   It was in our bones. It was just a matter of casting the parts at school usually and making up the party: 'Would you join us?' and 'Would you be the Black Knight?' or 'Would you be Bal-Hector?' or whatever it was. And ... you graduated from Wee Johnny Funny. I think I probably played Wee Johnny Funny when maybe I was six or seven, that would be 1921. And then I would do the other parts. The next part in seniority would be the Doctor, that was a relatively small part. And then perhaps ... Beelzebub. And then the two main parts that might've been played by Olivier or that calibre would be the Black Knight and Bal-Hector. ... So far as costume was concerned there was no relationship between the various parts. The only essential was that you had a black face, hence it was the Black Boys that they were called in Wigtownshire. So you had to have a black face and the rest of the costume had no reference whatsoever to the part. The costumes would be interchangeable insofar as everyone made up his own, and they were as I remember pretty weird and ridiculous, it just simply was disguise. I think I said in my note that the greatest accolade that any of the actors could be paid was to hear some of the listeners whispering during the play, 'Wha's that?' And then if you happened to hear that, then you knew that your make-up was absolutely perfect.

MM   Foolproof! The one who was dressed was the Doctor, he was always in a long black coat and had a little black bag with bottles and things. But he was always in a long black coat and I think a bowler hat. The others, as you say, were not setting themselves up to look like knights from Macedonia, but equally there was a class distinction. The village is about ten yards long, even so there was the top of the village and there was the foot of the village. And the top of the village boys did contrive some kind of, so to speak, costume. I can't remember what. But the foot of the village boys just turned their jackets outside in, having no store of clothes to raid, you know what I mean? So their dress was simply turning their jackets. And I can remember the lining of boys' jacket sleeves. ...

DL　It was a stock piece and probably on the night it was done by three or four different groups of boys, and therefore the village had to be divided up so that there wasn't a clash of two troupes arriving at the same time. And another aspect of it which was important was to get to the right people at the right time, in other words where there was most money. It was purely mercenary for boys, there was no question of entertaining their friends or trying out their hand at acting, it was to see how much money you could collect. And there were certain houses that were more worthwhile visiting than others. So within the bounds of dividing up the village that was probably kept reasonably strictly, but if there was one good house in your own section then that's the one you went for first. Unless you knew that the donor in that house didn't get back from work until half-past seven, so you went at half-past seven. And I think the other thing I mentioned about timing was that you didn't go out until the man was home from work and probably had his tea and was feeling more benign and generous than he would have done if you'd gone in just before he was about to eat. And all these things were –, they weren't discussed, they somehow were instinctive that you just knew where to go and when.

EL　How far out did you go?

DL　Well, the perimeter for one section of the village was a farm of Old Land.

MM　Half a mile out.

DL Yes, half a mile or so. And the perimeter on the south of the village was the mill house and probably down to the cottages –

MM Kirkland.

DL Yes, which is about the same distance. So that no more than a mile beyond the village end to end. ... I don't know how many houses we would do, and I think you're right, we didn't stay as late as ten thirty, maybe about nine. And we probably performed maybe a dozen or so houses, and of course we knew the ones that it wasn't even worthwhile knocking at the door because we knew that the reception was negative. ...

EL I wonder if you'd like just to say it through now, Mrs Muir? ...

MM Well, we can do it as a dialogue. ...

DL *Black Knight*
Here comes I the Black Knight,
Great King of Macedonia,
I have conquered many nations,
But Scotland is my fame.
When I first came to Scotland
My blood ran cold
To see old Scotland
So brave and so bold,
So frank and so free,
And I call upon Bal-Hector
To come and fight with me.

MM *Bal-Hector*
Here comes I Bal-Hector,
Bal-Hector is my name,
With sword and pistol by my side
I hope to win the game.

DL *Black Knight*
The game sir, the game sir,
It isn't in your power,
I'll slash you up in inches
In less than half an hour.
Fix! Charge!

MM		They fight.
DL		I've killed my brother, Jack.
		Is there a doctor in this town
		Can cure this deep and deadly wound?
MM	*Doctor Brown*	Here comes I old Doctor Brown,
		The best old doctor in the town.
DL	*Black Knight*	What can you cure, Doctor?
MM	*Doctor Brown*	All sorts, to be sure.
		The pain within, the pain without,
		If the devil's in I'll blow him out.
		A little to his nose, a little to his toes,
		Up Jack and fight again.
DL		And then it's Beelzebub, is it?
	Beelzebub	Here comes I Beelzebub,
		And over my shoulder I carry a clog,
		And in my hand a frying pan,
		I think myself a jolly old man.
MM	*Johnny Funny*	Here comes I wee Johnny Funny,
		A'm the man that lifts the money,
		A wee tin box below my airm,
		Tippence or thrippence'll dae me no hairm.
		End of play.

DL   That's it. And the other version to Johnny Funny was … the one about Christmas. …

> It's coming on for Christmas, the duiks are gettin fat,
> Please put a penny in the old man's hat.
> If ye havenae got a penny a halfpenny will do,
> And if ye havenae got a halfpenny, God bless you.

I'm not sure if they didn't alternate. … I remember clearly reciting that at some time [though] we never did any visiting at Christmas. …

EL   And you say you'd a special name for the night that you went out?

DL   Just called 'the Black Boys'.

MM   Black Boys' Night.

DL   And when you were making up your team, whoever was senior would ask the others, 'Are ye gaun oot on the Black Boys?' I don't even know that we used 'night' much.

MM   I thought it was 'Are ye gaun oot on Black Boys' Night?'

DL   The answer would be, 'Yes', or 'Aye, but I'm gaun wi John Smith's lot' – he had already been engaged, he'd already been contracted. ... Wee Johnny Funny ... has no connection with the narrative. I think he was there again for good commercial reasons. We felt that a wee boy might squeeze out an extra penny or two more than a big boy going round collecting, and I think that was probably part of why he was there. Maybe – I'm only thinking this now – maybe that in families, which were seldom less than five or six, whichever wee boy was the youngest in that family no doubt pleaded to be taken out, to be part of the fun. And Wee Johnny Funny might easily have started because of that. ... 'We'll take Jimmy and he can say Wee Johnny Funny.' I'm only thinking that now, I never thought of it before, but it's possible it could be that.

EL   What did he collect in?

MM   A tin box. ... They were of course all carrying turnip lanterns.

EL   Oh, they were?

DL   Yes.

MM   We had no street lighting or anything. The turnip lights had nothing to do with street lighting, but they did show a little light in entries and things. ...

EL   Did you get them out of a field?

DL   I was just going to say that was another prop that had to be acquired. I think we mostly stole them from the neighbours. I mean the farm land came right down to the village. Not that ... we had to steal them from the farms. My father always had some cattle ... and we would get our turnips certainly from our own stock for cattle-feeding.

MM   And the smell of them was awful, terrible, with the candle. ...

EL You were saying really as children you had no idea of whether the play was done anywhere else or not?

MM We knew our father and this uncle John who was virtually our grandfather in loco, you know, he served the part of grandfather to us because he was the eldest of a big family and our mother was the youngest and he was the patriarch, and he had done it.

EL Are the two of you remembering precisely the same years ... when you talk about the play? ...

DL Yes, well there's only a little more than a year between us. I, as I said, would probably go out when I was six, which was 1921. ...

MM You have done the Black Knight and Bal-Hector as well as Wee Johnny Funny?

DL Oh yes, I performed all roles.

MM I was an onlooker, you see. You know I was part of the – the women folk really were the audience.

DL I'm not sure thinking back whether I ever did the Doctor, I don't remember, but I've certainly done the other two.

EL You've done Wee Johnny Funny first, and then ... ?

DL Wee Johnny Funny first, and then Bal-Hector and ...

MM The Black Knight.

DL And the Black Knight. I don't think I remember doing the Doctor.

EL That's an interesting thing, actually, do you remember the names of the boys you did it with?

DL Yes, I don't think there was a team year after year, we changed. And, as I said, some years you wanted one particular boy to be in your lot but he has already committed himself to another one.

MM And then they left Kirkcowan school at eleven or so, to go to Newton Stewart, to the secondary, you see.

DL The number of boys who would perform on any Halloween night, that would perform this play, in total wouldn't be more than probably a dozen ...

MM Three sets or so ...

DL Yes, three or four. I think ... about four teams went round, so that's only about sixteen people, including Johnny Funny. And the number of boys that were available was restricted by the smallness of the community. ... A lot of [the boys] were country who didn't come in ... so ... there were probably only thirty boys of the right age to do this. ...

MM Living in the village.

EL You felt quite a distinction? ...

MM Oh yes, the country people were the ones from the outlying agricultural areas.

DL The country I would say, started at the two perimeters where we stopped at these two farms. Where there were no built-up houses, that was country. The village was simply the built-up area which extended less than a mile from top to bottom with this little one side street. ... The other interesting thing that just came into my head just now, I think I said that the schoolmaster was a fairly good bet on Halloween night. Now he was a fairly strict schoolmaster was Mr Cuthbert, and not only did we treat him with respect but the boys at any rate treated him with a little bit of fear, almost. But there was no fear whatsoever on Halloween night. There seemed to be just a subconscious truce on his part as well as our parts that this is not school, forget all about the discipline of school. And he entertained us and gave generously to Wee Johnny Funny. So that we didn't have any hesitation on going to his door. ...

MM Did people give you things besides money?

DL Yes, apples, oranges, nuts and I suppose some sweets, but for us money was the main one, and the rest were acceptable.

EL What did you carry them in?

DL Oh, we had capacious pockets and probably Johnny Funny had a wee bag just in case apples etcetera were given. And ... apart from the big tally at the end of the day, we had frequent tallies, at least two, during the night to see whether we were doing as well, whether the economy was as good this year as last. And I'm quite sure that each boy did as I did. If we discovered that the total collection at any given point was two and thruppence, then we made a mental calculation, how much of that was mine; it was very much mercenary.

MM   Cos a penny was a lot then. …

EL   Did you do anything special with the money that you collected?

DL   I don't know that we had any – I can't recollect ever having any project.

MM   And it wasn't for a charity or anything, it was for their pockets.

EL   Yes.

DL   No, I don't think I ever thought, well, after Halloween I will buy this or that. I just liked to get the money and have it to spend. I don't think I'd ever save it. …

EL   What did the Doctor do when he was curing?

MM   He got down on his knees. He opened his little black bag, which was always a bowler's bag.

DL   Yes.

MM   You know how bowlers have little pouchy bags, or they did.

DL   Green. ….

MM   You know a spring clip on the top and it had gussets at the end so that it was like a woman's pouched handbag wide enough to hold bowls. And he'd previously prepared this bag with bottles and tins and things. And so he got down and he opened this and he took out a bottle and held the bottle to the patient's nose and said, 'A little to his nose, and a little to his toes. Up Jack and fight again', that was all, wasn't it?

EL   Did he have any instruments like knives or anything?

MM   No, no.

DL   Just bottles and ointment.

EL   Was there anything in the bottle?

DL   No, I think it merely symbolical. I don't think – No, certainly not.

MM   The boy would've been –

DL   He'd just have a bottle and shake it at the patient's head and feet.

EL   It wasn't a doctor's sort of bag?

DL   I don't think there was any special bag required. You may remember a bowler's bag? ...

MM   It was designed to hold two round fat bowls, therefore it had gussets. It was made of leather.

DL   But I don't think it was essential, any bag that would be found.

MM   Yes, but my recollection is that they got their father's old bowler's bag, the shabby one. ...

EL   This must have been a popular village sport then?

MM   It was, yes.

DL   Bowling, yes, there were two village sports – well three – football, bowling and quoiting. ...

EL   Was there any singing in the play?

DL and MM   No.

EL   And did you do any other performance with it?

DL   No, we didn't. Others did. I mean Margaret mentioned it ...

EL   As well as the play? ... I mean the same people who did the play?

DL   No, no, they would go in, the players would go in and do their turn and go out.

MM   Take the money and go.

DL   Then perhaps we had to wait for a few minutes, we had to wait because there was another party in before us, either singing or reciting or something. And when we went, in five minutes there was another group, so that from the point of view of the listeners there was a stream of entertainment of one kind or another from six o'clock to nine.

MM   Because it was a community, you didn't turn away any children.

EL   And the girls were doing the other thing?
DL and MM   Yes.
EL   But some doors were shut?
DL   Yes, you could knock at a door and be greeted by 'Oh no, no, we've no time. We don't want to see you. We've had enough,' was the usual way out, because you couldn't argue with that. 'We've had enough tonight. Come back next year.'

9   David Laurie – Newton Stewart, 1926–1929

This reminiscence (SA1982.117B) was recorded, like [8], in Glasgow at the home of Mrs Margaret Muir, David Laurie's sister.

DL   I remember that it was a tradition in my mother's family. Now my mother's family name was Hunter. ... One of the aunts always began it by 'Here come I Galatians', and the other one began it ... 'Here comes I Bal-Hector, Bal-Hector is my name' – a little different. I also found that I remember this being done in Newton Stewart. There were two parts of Newton Stewart, one by the river called the Gorbals and further up called the Cottonmill for there was a cotton mill up there at one time. And they were done in both these parts, but the last time I can recall it was 1929. In 1930 I went into the bank and the annual balance was then on the 31st of October, and of course that was the night when it happened and I don't remember what happened after that. I was interested in [David Fergus's article in *The Scots Magazine*] because I once was the Black Knight, and I could remember 'Keep Silence all you gentlemen, Into your courts I say. My name it is the Black Knight, And I'll show you why', although that doesn't rhyme, but I can't remember it any better than that. 'Five of us are here, and merry boys we be. And we come into all your hooses for you to see. Your hooses for to see, sir. And pleasures for to have. And what you freely gie us We freely will noo tak', meaning 'now take', and I can't remember any more. ... So far as I recall there were only four people. There was Galatians, a Black Knight, a Farmer's Boy and a Doctor, but the action was virtually what was in the article. There were two aunts who really taught us this, and one was the eldest member of the family who was born in 1861. Her name was Margaret Hunter, she lastly was Mrs Wylie. The other one was Mary, we called her Aunt Doll, but she was a Mrs Roger, and she had gone to live in Motherwell where her husband was a solicitor, and she was the one who always began it:

> Here comes I Bal-Hector,
> Bal-Hector is my name.

There are two different versions. ...

EL   Do you think you went out several years doing the play?

DL   Yes, I can remember doing it when we lived in a house called Airlie, and we left Airlie in 1924 and we moved across the road and up to a house called Millburn. And I can remember doing it in both of these houses. ...

EL   And there were several of you in the family, brothers?

DL   Well, there were myself and my brother and there were two boys called Shaw who used to – It was a curious thing, the two houses were next door to each other. There were three boys and a girl and two were born during the First World War and two were born after, it was the same in both houses. So the two elder in each were boys and the four of us got together. And then there was another family called Kerr who lived in the Cottonmill, and there was a large family of them. And their father was an interesting man. He'd been many things, but when I knew him he came round with the baker's van and it was his family who did it up in what we call the Cottonmill. ...

EL   You say it was at Halloween?

DL   It was at Halloween, yes. It was always done at Halloween.

EL   Now you probably remember how everyone was dressed quite well?

DL   Yes, I remember that we were got up in a variety of things really. Galatians had a hessian sack with the two corners taken out, and he just went into that and it was tied around his neck. And he had some sort of weapon but I can't remember whether it was a sword or an axe – it was something in his hand. The Black Knight had a blue cross on this hessian bag and I had something on my head but I really don't remember the shape of it. I've got the feeling that it was something like a dunce's cap but I don't know. And I had a wooden sword . ... The Doctor was always all in black. I don't remember his head-dress but I remember he had a black coat on. What the Farmer's Boy was dressed in I don't know. My memory doesn't quite clarify that! Maybe he was just dressed as he normally was, but I couldn't be certain about that.

EL   Do you remember which of you took which parts? You were the Black Knight?

DL   Yes. The elder boy Shaw, David Shaw, he was tall and fair-haired and he was always Galatians. I was always the Black Knight. My brother was the Farmer's Boy because he was farming inclined and used to spend all his Saturdays out at a farm. The other boy Shaw, Hughie, was the Doctor. That was the sort of cast as it were.

EL   Now, how did the Doctor do his cure?

DL   Oh, now –

EL   There's usually a little bottle.

DL   Yes, yes, yes, yes.

EL   Did he have a bag? ...

DL   No, I think he came in with a sort of Gladstone bag thing. Oh yes, I can see him in his black coat which was far too long for him, and a Gladstone bag. What was in it I couldn't remember, and I don't remember what he had on his head, I'm sorry!

EL   Why did you go around the houses, do you think?

DL   Well, the tradition was, with us anyhow. We had a lot of relatives. We had two aunts who were married and an uncle who was the local photographer and the aunt had a toy shop and so on. And we always went to these three houses. I don't recall going anywhere else. We went to our own house, to the Shaws' and to the three relatives. Newton Stewart had a population of about under a couple of thousand then and we walked. We lived at one end and my aunt lived at the far end and the town was about a mile long. So I remember doing it in our own house, going to the Shaws, then my Aunt Meg, and then Aunt Lot's and then to Uncle Charlie's. ...

EL   What time of day was this?

DL   Usually after school. My mother was a great one for, 'You must be home early, you can't go out late'. And I remember particularly that it was nine o'clock, 'You must be home by nine o'clock'. Because, of course, once we got out we liked to stay out and by the time we had done the thing at these houses and I remember the two aunts particularly gave us money and nuts and apples. ...

EL   Where do you think you learned the words from? How did you learn the words?

DL   We were really, really – these aunts taught us it. Particularly the aunt who lived in Motherwell ... but she used to spend long periods in Newton Stewart. Indeed at Christmas my brother and I always went by train and we did all the pantomimes in Glasgow from there. She was the one who taught us quite a lot of it. But the old aunt, Aunt Meg, who was the head of the family, the oldest one of the Hunters, she was the one who really knew it off by heart.

EL   But it was a Newton Stewart tradition?

DL   And it was, I think, a Newton Stewart tradition and maybe something that had been in the Hunter family because there were twelve of the Hunter family, my mother was the youngest. ...

EL	Now you were older then your brother, is that right?
DL	I was the eldest, yes. And then my brother was about two years younger. And it was the same in the Shaw family, there was the eldest boy and the [second] one, and the other two were post-War and they were only five or six.
EL	The year you left school and began working you didn't do it?
DL	As I said, when I left and went into the bank the annual balance was the 31st of October and so we worked until about midnight, and so it was too late to do anything then.
EL	So did that mean that the group collapsed then?
DL	Yes, my feeling is that after 1929 it just disintegrated. I don't remember it happening at all. ...
EL	So that may just be the last year it was done?
DL	Yes.
EL	Did you ever see anyone else doing it?
DL	Yes, we saw this other family called Kerr who did it. But there too, I couldn't be sure of what happened. There was great rivalry because they were a large family scattered throughout the town and we had sort of – I wouldn't call it fisticuffs, but – we sort of ran at them with our swords, with our weapons when we saw them, more or less in fun!
EL	When you were out together at Halloween?
DL	When we were out, yes. And in these days there were a lot of other guiser children on the streets at Halloween, other children who were just dressed up. And, of course, there was a great vogue for turnip lanterns in those days, and all the children had turnip lanterns which they were carrying along the street.
EL	Sorry, I didn't quite understand you. The Kerrs, they were also doing the play, were they?
DL	The Kerrs, they did that play as well, and were dressed fairly similarly to what we were.
EL	Do you think they'd the same four characters? Do you know, at all?

DL I think they had. I wouldn't be positive but I think they did, yes. ...

>Keep silence all you gentlemen.
>Into your courts I say,
>My name it is the Black Knight
>And I'll show you why.
>Five of us are here
>And merry boys we be
>And we come into all your hooses
>For you to see,
>Your hooses for to see, sir,
>And pleasures for to have
>And what you freely gie us
>We freely now tak.

It's a funny ending but it's the best I can remember.

DL *[sic: EL]*

EL These words you were saying just now were actually what you said when you were the Black Knight?

DL Yes.

10 *David Kerr – Armadale, 1930–1932*

David Kerr, who worked as a builder before he retired, was born on 27 December 1919. I recorded him and his wife Ann, along with Audrey Bain, at his home in Armadale on 17 July 1993 (SA1993.072). Previously Mr Kerr had invited me to give a talk to a meeting of the West Lothian Heritage Society in Bathgate, and, when I played a recording of *Galoshins*, he recognised it and was happy to have his own reminiscences put on record. He had been taught the play by his father, James Stewart Kerr, who was born in Armadale in 1887, and he had never heard of its existence outside his own village. He had forgotten the opening speech, apart from the first line: 'Here comes in Sir John Monteith'. This character is present in the play from Inkerman (Hayward, 207–12) and his speech there runs:

> Here I come, Sir John Menteith,
> Ne'er a robber, nor a thief,
> Sir William Wallace I'll betray,
> Before the sun rises at break of day.

EL   What did you call it? Did you have a name for it?

DK   No, it didna have a name. It was just a play that we did when we were guising, and I first heard the play from my father. … It was a play about Sir William Wallace and Sir John Monteith and I think Sir John Monteith – he was the traitor, so at the start o the guising everybody had to boo when he came in, sort o melodramatic, and that was that. But when he taught it to my brothers and myself – they were younger than me – we would go out and do this play at various functions and things like that. For instance, the Church League of Friendship … had their dancing, so we made sure that we went there that night for oor guisin episode. And we did well, we went round wi the hat and we went round all these places. It was quite a good play. I think it's on the lines o the penny geggies that used to come where acting wis a kinna elaborate sort o thing. …

Will I jist go through it now and explain the play itself? Well, it's about William Wallace and Sir John Monteith and the players that are in it, the main players are these two and Doctor Brown and Wee Johnny Funny. That's the four main players, and if there's anybody else in the gang that night gaun oot guisin, they become retainers of William Wallace or John Monteith. Noo, the only thing about John Monteith, he enters first, and I've completely forgotten – I've racked my brains, and I've asked my brother, but I've forgotten the spiel that he came away wi, so it's no quite complete. But then he comes in wi his wooden sword and his helmet –

which was usually an ash-pan or a dust pan or something like that – and he comes in and struts aboot the stage and waves his wooden sword, and then in comes Sir William Wallace, and his spiel goes something like this:

> Here comes in Sir William Wallace,
> Sir William Wallace is my name,
> My sword and pistol by my side,
> I hope to win the game.
> The game sir, the game sir,
> It lies within my power,
> I'll cut you up in inches
> In less than half an hour.

And he's sorta sparring wi Sir John Monteith, ye see. So the two o them fight. They get their wee wooden swords out and they fight and the retainers on either side, they're battering on the side tae spin that yin oot a wee bit and make it a kinna realistic fight. And then of course they aa injure each ither and they faa down dead, the whole lot o them! And then the next player that comes in is old Doctor Brown, and he's dressed in his wee bowler hat and his spats and his wee black bag, ye see, wi his magic potions. So he comes runnin in and:

> Here comes in old Doctor Brown,
> The best old doctor in the town.

And the audience, there's a plant there usually, or an MC, he says: What can you cure?

The Doctor says: All sorts!

Audience What's all sorts?

Doctor A wee bottle o inky pinky, wi the hee gee gee [with 'g' pronounced as in 'go'] and the ho go go that all the people fancy.

The audience, the plant:

> Give them all a snuff!

So the Doctor goes round wi his wee magic bottle and gives them all a sniff at the bottle, ye see. So of course they gradually stretch and wake up and stand up, and then they sing. And I havenae a very good voice, but here, I'll try. Here's the wee song that they sing, all in the line, like a barber's-shop choir:

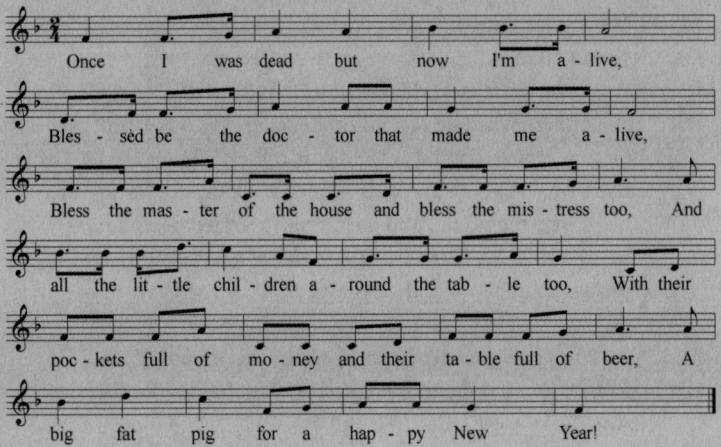

Once I was dead but now I'm a-live,
Bles-sèd be the doc-tor that made me a-live,
Bless the mas-ter of the house and bless the mis-tress too, And
all the lit-tle chil-dren a-round the tab-le too, With their
poc-kets full of mo-ney and their ta-ble full of beer, A
big fat pig for a hap-py New Year!

And then there's a big elaborate bow after that, and that's that. That's the play really finished. And then in comes in this wee, the wee-est laddie in the company usually, dressed in his big Kilmarnock bunnet and his long troosers, long shorts anyway, and he says:

> Here comes in Wee Johnny Funny,
> The best wee man tae gaither the money,
> Lang hairy pooches doon tae his knees,
> Tuppence or thruppence or three bawbees.

And that's it. So the only thing is that I forgot the Sir John Monteith spiel. ... Jist 'Here comes in Sir John Monteith'. ... After that he had a wee spiel like Wallace's spiel, you see. ...

EL   So did you have a part that you usually played yourself?
DK   Well, the reason that I remember – I was the oldest in my family, ye see, so of course naturally I played the hero, Sir

	William Wallace. And I thought my brother who played Sir John Monteith would have remembered his spiel, but he didna.
EL	Which brother was that?
DK	The one in Canada.
EL	What's his name?
DK	Jimmy. James.
EL	And who were the others that took part in this?
DK	Well, there was one or two in the gang. My other brother, he was younger so he got the part o Wee Johnny Funny, but there was others in that guisin gang. Dick Coard, for instance, he played the fiddle, and we'd quite a varied programme besides this. We would sing and dance and tell stories as well as that. So we'd do a pretty good wee show for oor money.
EL	And so your younger brother, what's his name?
DK	Robert. He would take the part of Wee Johnny Funny; he was the wee-est laddie, ye see.
EL	And what about Doctor Brown?
DK	It'd be one of the others – either Dick Coard or Allie MacDonald, you know, some of the boys that we ran about wi.
EL	How old were you when you were doing it?
DK	I reckon I would be aboot ten, or eleven, round aboot that age; ten, I think.
EL	Had you ever seen other boys doing it?
DK	No that play, no, no. The only one – well, I heard another man, an adult, say some o the verses in that wee play in Armadale, from Armadale, but the only one really other than that was my father.
EL	So who was this other man?
DK	He's dead now; he was one o the last generation. I've forgotten his name, too. No, I cannae remember it.
EL	And how was it that you came to hear him saying it?
DK	Well, he was in – in fact my father owned some houses at the top o the Mill Road in Armadale and he was his factor,

so he was in doing a bit o business at that time. And I heard the two o them, you know, talking about – reminiscing, and talking about the old times – and this was one o the things that came up. And this old guy he came away wi some o the verses along wi ma father, so he did know the thing, but where he had heard it, I don't know. Or how my father heard it, I don't know either.

EL Did your father belong to Armadale?
DK He was born in Armadale but his parents, well, his mother's family had farmed in the Uphall and Broxburn area. ...
EL So you entirely learned it from your father?
DK Yes, yes.
EL And he told you the actions as well?
DK And he would do the actions with us, yes.
EL And *all* of you died?
DK Aye, they all died.
EL Apart from Doctor Brown!
DK Apart from Doctor Brown. ... All the retainers who were in the fight between Wallace and Sir John Monteith, they died. ...
AB So was this a thing that was done by most of the boys in the town? ...
DK Well, guising was the usual thing. We earned a wee bit o money. I think on that occasion we all got aboot sixty pence – aboot sixty pence each. That was quite a good night's work, you know, when you consider that you got a penny at a time.
EL You weren't going around people's houses, were you?
DK Yes.
EL Oh, you were. Doing this?
DK Yes.
EL And you also did it for an evening's kind of entertainment in a hall?
DK No. If there was a dance on, for instance, amongst the young people, we made sure we went there because that was

	a good source of money. If they went round wi the hat among a crowd in the hall, we did quite well oot o our evening's guising.
EL	So then you did it in the hall?
DK	We did it in the hall or in people's houses.
EL	Now, what time of year?
DK	At Halloween. …
EL	And what time of day did you start?
DK	As soon as it got dark. And we made sure that we had places to go. For instance, we all went to our relatives. That was a surefire invitation to come in and do your piece. But I must say we were good. We were a good show – good value for money. Nowadays they just come in and they've got the American idea, trick or treat. You go in and you haud the people to ransom and ye get yer apple or whatever. But we really put on a good wee show.
AB	Were you ever given anything else apart from money?
DK	Apples, nuts, oranges, you know, that sort of thing. Oh, there was a lot o the houses where they just gave you a penny or two, for they hadna much money themselves, but ye always got an apple or an orange or something like that which ye shared out at the end.
EL	Now I think you talked about a guising gang, did you?
DK	Well, just young chaps that hung about at school together and things like that. It wisna anything that we kept up, you know, we came together for this. Some of us could play the fiddle or the mouth organ or the Jew's harp, you know. So we'd take them and put on the show.
EL	It was all boys, was it?
DK	All boys, oh, aye. Well, we were sorta more or less segregated in these days, you know. In fact the lassies, they were better at these rhymes with their skipping games and their ball games and things like that. The laddies had a few o these things but I think it was the girls that were the best at these bairn rhymes, sort of.

EL   Apart from this group of you that were taught by your father, other people in the village were going around at Halloween. What were they doing?

DK   Well, they would jist sing or dance or tell a wee story or a joke or whatever. I think they were usually quite good.

EL   Was there a special rhyme?

DK   No, no, I don't remember any specially.

EL   Did you have a wee Halloween rhyme?

DK   Aye, that was another one of my father's.

> Halloween, tick, tick, teen,
> Three wee witches on the green,
> Yin black an yin green,
> An yin crying 'Halloween'.

EL   … And there was a New Year one as well, was there?

DK   New Year. Oh, aye. …

> Christmas is coming and the pigs are getting fat,
> Please put a penny in the old man's hat,
> If you hivna got a penny, a halfpenny will do,
> If you hivna got a halfpenny, God bless you!

EL   Now, when was that said? Do you remember?

DK   Well, that would be at Christmas and New Year. That time of year, I would think.

EL   Do you remember doing that?

DK   No. No, that's another one o my father's. Oh, he had a few.

EL   Was there a New Year one at all? I think you said 'Rise up auld wife'?

DK   Oh yes, that yin.

> Rise up auld wife and shake yer feathers,
> Dinna think that we are beggars,
> We are bairns come oot tae play,
> Rise up auld wife and gie's oor Hogmanay.

And of course ye got yer wee glass of wine or ginger wine or blackcurrant wine or something.

EL   Do you remember doing that one, then?

DK We often said that one at Hogmanay time. ...
EL And when exactly did you say that?
DK Well, just in a family gathering, in that sort of context. We didnae go out and say it at houses or anything like that, but in the family some of us when we were sitting round the table sometimes we'd jist break into that yin. My father would probably lead it off too.
EL Did that have a tune?
DK No. ...
EL I wonder if I could ask you, Ann. You've seen this done, have you?
AK Yes, when we were younger, yes. Eh, that one verse about Sir John Monteith ... 'The game sir, the game sir, it is within my power'.
DK No, that's Wallace's speech.
AK No, I don't remember these as well as David. ...
DK Of course, I passed on this to my own family.
AK And our boys, they've forgotten it. We used to teach them when they were small, but they don't – they're not interested.
EL So did they go out at Halloween, your boys?
AK Yes.
DK Yes, but not with this play, there was a break after me. The next generation werena quite so interested, you see, and they were –
EL So you taught them the play but they didn't go out?
DK They didnae pick it up. ...
EL Do you remember, say, how the doctor was dressed? Can you tell us?
AK Oh, it was usually an urchin type –
DK No, the Doctor.
AK Oh, the bowler hat, the Doctor, the bowler hat, and his wee white rubber collar and the long three-quarter trousers. And his wee black bag, wi the magic potion in the wee black bag. He had this magic potion to bring them all alive. Quite an important man, was Doctor Brown!

AB	Did they ever wear their jackets outside in or anything like that?
AK	Oh no, it was authentic, you had to dress properly, oh no! No, the way the doctors would. And they had their wooden swords and –
EL	And how were the fighters dressed?
AK	Oh, just their shirts and trousers and a belt, that was it.
EL	And you were going to describe – was it Johnny Funny?
AK	Oh, he was just a wee urchin type.
DK	He was jist a wee urchin, wi his long shorts and his faither's old jaiket wi the long pooches.
AK	And an auld cap on, back to front.
EL	Yes. What were these pouches, exactly?
DK	His pockets, long pockets. It wis his faither's jacket, ye see. On a wee laddie his jackets would go away doon his ankles, and the pockets were nice and deep to hold all the apples and oranges and nuts as well as the money.
EL	So they were just the normal jacket pockets?
DK	It wis jist his faither's jacket but on him it looked long.
AK	'Long pooches.' …
EL	Do you remember the New Year one that David was saying?
DK	'Rise up auld wife and shake your feathers' …
AK	Oh yes. … That was quite a common one, everybody said that.
EL	And when did you hear this?
AK	This was in the night before New Year, you did this. Go round the doors to get your New Year apple or orange or whatever that wis going. …
EL	So did you go out twice in the year?
AK	Twice, yes. Usually just to relatives at New Year time …
EL	What would happen, do you remember, if Halloween was on a Sunday?
DK	That's a good question.
AK	I don't ever remember. I don't think we would've been allowed to do it. Believe it or not, they were quite strict

	about what you could do on a Sunday and what you couldn't do. No, I can't imagine children then going to a house on a Sunday to do that.
EL	David was saying you'd go out after dark at Halloween?
AK	Oh yes, it had to be dark because you had your torch.
EL	And what about Hogmanay?
AK	Hogmanay was more for the grown-ups, Hogmanay was more a grown-up thing.
EL	But you did go round as children?
AK	We did aunts, or just immediate neighbours, but that was more a grown-up ceremony. And ye'd go to the door then, but ye were well in bed before twelve o'clock.

11 *John Anderson – Falkirk, 1905–1908*

John M. Anderson, an accountant, had written a piece called 'The Galoshuns and the Guisers' for *The Edinburgh Tatler* in 1976 and sent it to Paul Smith when he appealed for information in *The Scottish Field*. Following up on this, I recorded Mr Anderson in his home in Falkirk on 7 November 1980 (SA1980. 100). Mr Anderson was born in February 1900 and recalled seeing the play when he was very young. The performances had adult direction and were much more elaborately organised than usual. They took place at both Halloween and New Year and Mr Anderson noted in a letter he sent to me just after our recording session: 'The Hallowe'en Play differed from the Xmas or rather New Year Play in that as a Prelude the Talking Man recited Burns's "Hallowe'en" but omitted the Prelude at the New Year.' He also noted that in the procession between performance locations each of the two warriors was followed by a servant who 'wore a false face attached to the head by elastic' and carried the knight's shield. Mr Anderson distinguished the false faces worn by the followers from the masks which were carried, not worn, by some of the principals. He commented: 'The Knights carried masks on staves. Before the duel each knight exchanges his mask for his shield.' The Talking Man also carried a mask which he discarded inside the room. Doctor Brown, who was carrying a black bag, did not have a mask. In his follow-up letter, Mr Anderson gave the scheme of the procession as: the boy with the whistle; the pair Talking Man and Singing Man; the pair Sir William Wallace and King Robert the Bruce; the pair of their servants; the pair Doctor Brown and the dancing girl; Johnny Funny; and three young dancing girls or boys. The Singing Man, who also carried a mask 'which he discarded when singing', makes an interesting counterpart to the Talking Man, but it is clear that he was the soloist who performed after the play and did not have a part in the play proper. In his *Edinburgh Tatler* article, Mr Anderson noted that 'the combatants were dressed in knight's armour with wooden shields and swords', and in his letter to Paul Smith of 28 March 1977 he noted that Robert the Bruce wore a paper crown. In this letter he mentioned that the performances took place 'in the poorer part of Falkirk, where there were numerous tenements housing working-class families'. In the recording session he spoke of living as a boy in Grahamstown, about half a mile from Falkirk High Street.

Although Mr Anderson could not sing the revival lines, he identified the tune as that of the chorus of 'Oor guidman come home at een' (Bronson, 4.99, no. 3), which was a song his mother sang (cf. the same tune indication in Falkirk in Dale 1925). Mr Anderson's words are set here to that tune:

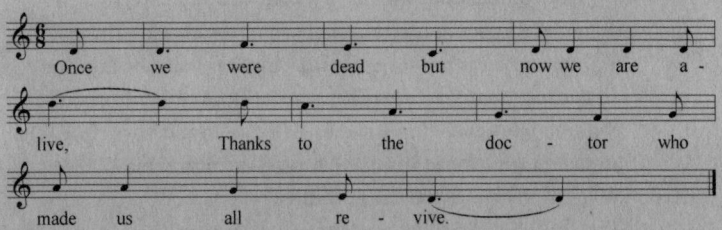

JA [The *Galashins*] came to be played as part of the enjoyment of the New Year and Christmas, but in my day it had gone a stage further and there was a version of the play done for Halloween, so we had the children playing it at Halloween for a week, and then it was played for a week just after Christmas before the New Year. Remember that Christmas in my childhood was not a holiday for the workmen, no. The shops themselves were open on Christmas Day. The children, however, received one day's holiday from the school, but a day or so later for the New Year we had about a fortnight's holiday, so of course all the enjoyment and the pleasure-loving activities centred around the New Year rather than Christmas. ... The play itself was done in the old-fashioned tenement kitchen, and [in] a tenement kitchen in Falkirk ... for the most part the sink was in front of the window ... with the presses alongside, one for dishes and one for food. ... [The room had a] recess and a bed [was] put in there and the curtains would be drawn across it during the daytime. ... We have to remember there was no electric light, a gas lamp swung from the mantelpiece across on a swivel so it could be pushed a little out of the way if wanted. We'd the old-type range or fireplace there, certainly with an open fire burning. Then following that we had the arrangement made with the children that they would be acceptable in particular houses in the district and the other neighbours all called in that night as well in order to see the play, so it was quite an event. They generally had what one might call a two-show night, two houses in the one evening and they pretty well done the district in a week, that would be about – they'd do it about perhaps ten times. Friday night it was not done at all because that was the night for the Boys' Brigade and the children who played in it were nearly all in the Boys' Brigade and certainly would not have missed it for any play.

EL What kind of age were the children?

JA The children varied in age from about twelve years of age

	down to about seven or eight years of age, the older boys would be about twelve, perhaps less, maybe about eleven, but they were big boys as I remember them, when I would be about six. ...
EL	Was it all boys? Ever any girls?
JA	Yes, usually we had one girl who was permitted to act in it and she did a dance, either the Highland fling or the sword dance. Sometimes she sang but not very often. It was almost entirely a boys' affair. ... Now, I come now to the play itself and the staging. The people themselves, the ladies all sat on both sides of the fireplace right across almost to the doorway, leaving an opening for the people to come from the corridor in, and the men stood behind, and sometimes opened – as it was very warm there – opened the door into the larder, or somewhere, and stood in the doorways. Remember it was a full audience, there was no question of that, and the children went on the top of the bed, knelt down and they could get a front view because on the mat in front of the fireplace the whole play was done. Now you have the actual scenic view of it and you can see for yourself that everybody saw everything connected with the play.
EL	A splendid picture you're giving me!
JA	Now, well, I'm hoping, I'm trying to make it a picture of the conditions. Now when the play was ready to begin the light was turned off, the gas-light feature, and swivelled back out of the way, and the only light in the kitchen where the play was held, now the theatre if we call it that, was in darkness except for the fire, which in a winter's night was of course glowing with the old coal – there was no smokeless fuel in those days, it was coal and wood – and sometimes pieces of wood were thrown on to give a brighter effect to it. If the moon was up, the window blind was lifted to its full and the light of the moon sometimes came in and gave a kind of eerie effect, remembering that the children were all done up with those masks and had a somewhat frightening effect,

especially to the very young children. Swords that were used were of wood and quite a lot of effort was done to make sure that the battle was fought properly. An old boxer who had a boxing ring quite near at hand in his garden and taught boys how to box, and how to fence, and how to play single sticks over their heads: he taught the boys how to fence properly with the sticks which had been made into swords, and indeed I think he must have loaned them as well. And we had also a very fine elocutionist who helped with the cantatas in the town, a man called Mr Winchcomb. He took those children and saw that they could state their lines properly and act it in a proper manner, so don't get away with the idea that it was just a kid on, it was a properly done play, as well done as would have been on a large stage. Now the first introduction to the play is the Talking Man and he arrives at the door and knocks at the door explaining to the lady of the house that they are not beggars, that they have come to play their play and, if they didn't believe them, they would go away again, and of course they are invited into the house. Then the Talking Man takes up his place in the middle of the mat, and later on he takes a side part, just like some of the modern plays, in which the Talking Man tells about something that's going to be done, so he took in hand to tell you about what was happening as it was going on, and the first bit of course is that he gets the poker:

> Stir up the fire be on your mettle,
> For inside this house tonight there'll be
> a battle.

And here it differed with different sets of people. The one that we were most associated with had Sir William Wallace and Robert the Bruce as protagonists, but there were others we had. Bob Slasher is another one which is mentioned in *The Falkirk Mail* [Dale, 1925], and I think there are even different names in the actual printed copy of the play. It had obviously not been the printed copy that the children worked

	from, but from an old tattered copy that had been found at school probably and been handed down.
EL	Did you ever see this copy?
JA	Yes, they all had a copy of this, hand-written, so that they could take their actual cue in their parts, you see, and the Talking Man had kept this in his hand – the children didn't – but kept it in his hand in order to prompt them, because you always found that some child or other forgot a part, and he prompted them in a word because it was just allowable that this could be done. And then the – after the battle has been fought then one of the persons is killed. … They ask if there is a doctor in the town and of course in comes Doctor Brown, the best wee doctor in the town, and he is asked what he can do and he tells about the various things he can do and – but he is asked, can he resurrect a dead man, bring him to life again. Oh, he says, he can try, and he does try, by pinching the nose and touching the ears and doing all kinds of things to the boy an, if it is Sir Robert the Bruce, he sits up and he comes alive, and of course the other children, who have not yet taken part in the play, come in and then they'd all dance round about and have a sing-song to the man who was able to do this. Now you would understand that this did not take very long, and all children's plays, as a matter of fact you can hardly hold the attention for more than ten or fifteen minutes and they took about that to do it. But following that there was brought in the swords which had been used, were laid down and a girl came in and danced the sword dance. In our case there was a lady there who knew how to play the violin and she played the violin for the person doing the sword dance. Sometimes for an encore she would do the Highland fling. When I tell you that she danced those in her bare feet, it was not just done in the highest of style, but it was quite interesting because all the people knew the dances and gave her a great cheer. Then, following that, a boy would give a song and this was some-

what different in different places. At Halloween it was not done at all, but at Christmas time the song was one of the pantomime songs and the one I can remember of most was about someone who was, 'Skinny Malinky was so thin, he was thin as a hose pipe', and I always thought that was very, very funny.

EL Can you remember the tune of that, can you sing that?

JA No, I can't remember the tune of that one, and 'Our goodman come hame' was the tune that they sung when they, when the children all went round about, but I can't remember that about Skinny Malinky but there's bound to be a record of it somewhere because it was quite a popular song, and the man who originated it would be Funny Frame. ... At that time his posters appeared in Falkirk with a huge eggshell of a body and very tiny legs and a very tiny head and he was known as Funny Frame. Indeed he was the forerunner of the Scottish comedians of today. ... His two songs – a song 'To the Paris exhibition, I'll go back on no condition', was one of them, and about a polis man – going to the West End Park and kinda dressed up and says 'Ma man's a polis man, an I'm going to meet him in the West End Park', – those were quite favourites of that time. ... I am now going to give you the play much as I can remember it. You have to remember, of course, I didn't actually act in the play myself, I was only about six years of age, but I remember much of it because I was so keen at that time. Now the children arrived at the door, the leader playing a penny whistle, and they were marched in the order of a little company of soldiers with of course all the people round about, and they knocked at the door which – that they had been pre-arranged to have the play. When they knocked at the door, the lady of the house opened the door herself and was greeted with the following words:

> Rise up auld wife and shake your feathers,
> Dinna think that we are beggars,

> We are but bairnies oot to play,
> Rise up an gie's our Hogmanay,
> And I will show you the prettiest thing
> That ere was seen at Christmas time.

Now it was then – took a little time to arrange in the corridors to have the various masks and things put on. Following this, the Talking Man takes up his place in the middle of the mat and in front of the fire and starts off to say:

> Stir up the fire be on your mettle
> For inside this house will be a battle.
> If you don't believe a word I say
> I'll send my players all away.

Of course everybody clapped and it was continued. He then proceeds to introduce Sir William Wallace and in swashbuckling style declares that he is the rightful king of Scotland. Robert the Bruce then appears and challenges Wallace, 'I am the king of Scotland, the true king of Scotland', so with that both draw their wooden swords and, having learned how to fence properly, gave a good display of a battle in which Sir William Wallace was slain. Robert the Bruce is grief-stricken, but is told to cheer up by the Talking Man who calls for a doctor. Finally the Doctor arrives, he has a black bag, of course, and the little black hat which made him quite different from the others, and we have him saying – the Talking Man says of him:

> Here comes in old Doctor Brown
> The best old doctor in the town.

And the Talking Man says: What can you cure?
and Doctor Brown answers:

> The rout, the tout, the ringworm and the scurvy.

Talking Man says: Can you cure a dead man?
Doctor Brown: I can try.

Removing a medicine bottle from his bag the doctor pulls the cork, kneels beside the corpse and, suiting his actions to his words, says,

> Put a little to his nose, put a little to his tongue,
> Rise up Sir William and give us a song.

Sir William rises and they all join hands singing, but before that the other members of the cast come in to join and make a ring at which they all dance round about Sir William Wallace and Robert the Bruce who stand in the middle shaking hands. Now the song had something to do with the words 'Once we were dead but now we are alive', I just can't remember the rest of the words of it. I think a line was 'Thanks to the doctor who made us all revive' but I wouldn't be quite sure about that last line because – Why I say that was I always thought this to be a little curious as only one person had been revived, but I liked the tune, of the chorus from 'Oor guidman come home at een'.

EL Can you sing that then?

JA I couldn't sing that, I'm sorry. ... As a singist, I'm not a success. ... After the revival song it was usual for the dancer to dance the sword dance using the wooden swords and accompanied by the fiddler, the soloist followed with one of the favourite music-hall successes, which I talked about before. ... At the end of this singing, remembering that each of them had an encore so you have the dancers doing two dances and the singer giving an encore, we had gone the length of about half-an-hour's time, and then the Talking Man called in Wee Johnnie Funny who wore his father's jacket which makes the point that:

> Here comes in Wee Johnny Funny,
> The best wee man to draw the money.
> Lang lang pouches down to his knees,
> A penny a tuppence or three bawbees.

... Now the children were ready to leave, got on their coats in the hall and as they left they made a blessing to the mistress of the house after having had a bag of apples, oranges, pieces of cake and lemonade and all this served up to them and a little bit of money that the Johnny Funny had picked up, which wasn't very much if it was divided between eight or ten persons. ... And as they left the house and said thank you, the Talking Man again says:

> Bless the maister of this hoose, the mistress bless also
> And all the bonnie bairnies that roond the table go.

And then they came outside; if it was downstairs they walked downstairs, and formed themselves into a small company again, the boy playing the tin whistle, [and] marched off to the next house to play the same play again somewhere else. That is as it was done and I'm sorry that I can't remember the complete play. ...

EL   Now what did the Johnny Funny collect the money in? Would he have something?

JA   Yes, he collected the money in his hat. He had an old hat and a rather curious thing was it was an old tall hat. Now you have to remember that in Scotland at communion time ... no man would go to church if at all possible without what we call the swallow-tail coat and the tall hat. Father's tall hat was so tall that I can remember him getting two inches cut off the top of it to bring it more up-to-date and this – naturally a number of old silk hats were knocking around, and the boy that came in with the tall hat and his father's jacket, which was 'down to his knees', of course, was quite correct, came in and brought the silk hat and you had to put your money into it. It was chiefly the men who put the money in at the back. It was not the wives, who didn't have any money in their pockets as a rule. So that was how the money was collected, but it wasn't a great deal. I should say that if they collected a shilling or one-and-six-pence it would be as much as they collected, money, but they did get a big slice of cake an a great piece of shortbread and oranges, apples and all the usual things that were – dates, a box of dates was sometimes put in. But the shortbread was rather curious, the shortbread in those days in the Falkirk district was not bought in fingers but you sent it, your butter and sugar, into the co-operative society and they baked it for you – remembering very few of the houses had baking ovens, good baking ovens – and the baking was done in the co-operative society for them. They were in large pieces and it was not considered the done thing to cut shortbread, it had to be broken with the fingers so that perhaps half a cake for these children was broken and put into the soft paper and put into the bag which they'd taken with them. ...

EL What sort of bag was the shortbread put in? ...

JA It wasn't really a bag I should say, it was a big basket, it was the old-fashioned basket which ... was big enough to carry four to five loaves so it gives you an idea of what the size of it was, and the shortbread was put into a piece of soft paper, that thin white soft paper, and the same thing was done with the cake, and a large slab again, and the cake was usually cut into so many pieces and sliced so that the children could have them, but the distribution of these I don't know anything about how it was distributed afterwards because I didn't see. I only saw them actually getting the things.

EL Did you see this little procession with the person playing the whistle?

JA Oh yes, all the children were standing waiting at the door, waiting on the procession coming along to the house, and when it came along to the house, we, somebody would go shouting, 'They're coming, they're coming!'. ...

EL What did you call the group of people when you said, 'They're coming'?

JA The players.

EL The players.

JA Yes, the players are coming. ...

EL Do you remember how the boy playing the tin whistle was dressed?

JA Yes, yes, I could remember. He had on a red pointed hat and I do remember one thing, he had a belt around – I think it would be a Boys' Brigade belt – tied round his middle, and he played this and he had a neckerchief. ... All the moulders in the district had a red [one] with white spots, you know, the old neckerchiefs. They used to tie round about their neck at night when they came off the cast, it was so hot and they tied this round their neck, but in the mornings they used to tie it round their waists when they went off to work. Now this would be tied, of course, as we now think of as the Boy Scout knot, the double knot and the drop, that was how it was tied. So I can remember this red and white and the red hat just pointed up, tilted a little on the angle, just to make him odd and the belt ... so he looked quite a smart type of boy, something just a wee bit out of the ordinary. The others, of course, were quite different because they were dressed up with all these masks and things and different dresses on to suit the masks. And the little girl she came along just in the middle and, what I can't understand, why she didn't come dressed with her kilt and all on, but she didn't; she came just with a plain skirt on and her bare legs and danced in her bare feet.

EL And were they wearing the masks when they were in the street?

JA Yes, ... and that drew the crowd.

EL And was it a procession, one behind the other?

JA No, they were in twos and there would be about, I'd say, ten of them in all. The leaders, of course ... you had Wallace, Bruce, Talking Man and Doctor Brown, you see, and you had the dancer and the singer – you can begin to see how you could get eight or ten in – and the others were the younger ones who came in and sung afterwards. ...

EL Were they in the procession too?

JA At the end of the procession, they made up the end of the procession. ...

EL Now the boy with the whistle, was he walking on his own or did he have a partner?

JA He was on his own.

EL Yes.

JA He was on his own, he led the – ...

EL Now, how was the Talking Man dressed?

JA Yes, he was dressed in what would be known today as a Homburg hat ... and ... the one I can remember quite well, he had a black velvet jacket, it looked like a kind of smoking jacket ... with a belt set round about it, and he was done with linen collar and tie which was at that time not an ordinary tie but a bow tie, keeping the style with him, and he had linen cuffs, but remember that linen cuffs were quite common. I could never go to church on a Sunday as a child of six year old without linen cuffs and also an Eton collar. ...

EL And when do you think you saw this play?

JA Oh, certainly between 1905 and 1908 I saw it on several occasions, certainly on one occasion at Halloween but mostly at the Christmas time or just after Christmas as I've explained before, between that and the New Year.

EL Were these children that you knew? Were they friends of yours?

JA Some of the children I knew but not all of them. Remember that they were two or three years older than myself for the most part, it would be only be the very younger children that I would know and I just don't remember. The only one I do remember o is the dancer, who was a half-cousin of my own, a good reason for remembering her. ...

EL Do you think the children organised this themselves?

JA No, the organisation was not done by themselves.

12 *Robert Hendry – Camelon, 1922–1927*

Mr Hendry responded to my appeal in *The Scots Magazine* in January 1982 and I recorded him on 10 June 1982 at his home in Upper Largo, Fife (SA1982.114). When he performed in the play he was living in Camelon, Stirlingshire, which lies to the west of Falkirk. Robert Hendry's father, David, who was a polisher in the iron foundry, had performed in the play as a boy at Stenhousemuir, two or three miles to the north. Mr Hendry's use of the word 'baksheesh' for a gift to beggars is explained by the fact that he had spent time in India, as he mentioned at a later point in the interview when discussing customs.

RH   Well when we were youngsters we went out guising, always on Halloween only. But my father, he thought that we were very amateurish and not doing enough for what he reckoned was guising. And he taught me this play of *Galatians*, which I knew nothing about, and I'd never heard of it. And he gave us the various parts, which I think there were four or five of us in it. Nothing very long because the idea was to get out and into as many houses as you could in the evening to get a few pence from each one as we went, that was all. ... He had advised me not to be Galatians, but the other bloke who did the killing rather than – Galatians being prone on the floor was less able to get away if somebody was – some of the families were a bit obstreperous about things, you know. But we never had any occasion like that. But according to my father, sometimes they didn't get a very pleasant reception, after having been invited into the house, you know. If they weren't performing properly, or up to what the people thought was the standard, they just chased them, you see. But that never happened to us at any time. ...

EL   Well, perhaps we should take it a little bit from your father's point of view first of all. What did he tell you that he had done, as far as you can recall?

RH Well, he just told us what they had done. ... He was advising me and quoting the lines to me – he never wrote them down, I just had to memorise them – and then get the parts off and teach the other boys of my own age who were going to do it, you see.

EL Did you learn it first and then teach the others?

RH I learned it from him and then I had to teach them, you see. So more or less I knew it all, but I don't remember it all today, I don't think.

EL Well, perhaps you'd like to run through what you do remember, just perform it?

RH Well, we started off having got into the house to do our performance – we were all dressed up of course in various costumes, nothing very fancy, but we thought they were – and started off with Galatians walking in and saying,

> Here comes in Galatians,
> Galatians is my name,
> With sword and pistol by my side
> I hope to win the game.

Then I would say,

> The game sir, the game sir,
> It's not within your power
> I'll cut you up in slices
> In less than half an hour.

And he says,   You sir? Yes, me sir.
And he said,   Take out your sword and try, sir.

So then we drew our swords and had a bit of a sword battle, and finally he was defeated and collapsed on the floor. Then I'd turn to – there was a fifth chap there – and say:

> Run around the town
> And roust out the good old Doctor Brown

to come and fix this fella. So then he'd walk out and then Doctor Brown would walk in and do a bit of medication to Galatians and get him on his feet again. And then in came wee Johnny Funny, the man that takes in all the money, with long, long pooches doon tae his knees, for ha'pennies, pennies and wee bawbees. And then we did a bit of a song and so on and got a collection if there was anything going, you see, and that was it, you know. But there was more to it than that from my father's point of view, but I can't remember exactly what it was. I hadn't thought about it till I saw the airticle. ...

EL What were the actual words that wee Johnny Funny comes in with? What does he say?

RH Well, he comes in:
> Here comes in wee Johnny Funny
> I'm the man that takes in all the money.
> Wi' long, long, pooches doon tae my knees,
> For ha'pennies, pennies and wee bawbees.

That was it, ye see. And he was always a small fella; you used to get a smaller fella to do that.

EL Were the rest of you all in the same class?

RH All the same age, same age group, even Johnny Funny. We jist got a small fella to do it.

EL Well now, you know quite a bit about how you were dressed up. Could you just run through all the characters and what they wore?

RH Well, we basically tried to get clothes – they were usually just some of our fathers' long trousers ... to try and get a sort of military uniform. It didn't work very much, you know, but mostly just dressed up, and faces coloured up with black stuff and so on, usually soot more than anything else. To be sort of brigands more than anything else, I think, or military personnel. We didn't know why because there was no history behind it as far as I know. But Doctor Brown, he had a Gladstone bag, and my father had one, so he used to lend us the Gladstone bag for the Doctor's medicine bag, with a few bits of knives and forks and things like that in it.

EL Did he use those during the action?

RH Yes, he'd go through the action with that lot. I remember a

	wine glass as well for supposed to be giving him a drink of potion. Medicine bottle as well, with nothing in it, but that was the idea.
EL	So the glass and bottle were in the bag?
RH	Were in the bag, and knives and forks we had for his surgical instruments, sorta business.
EL	How was the Doctor dressed?
RH	Oh, he was all dressed up with good clothes on. Usually with his father's bowler hat, or his soft hat or something like that. He was a real professional gentleman as opposed to us being sort o soldier types, as it were. That was really the point there.
EL	So, a bowler hat and –
RH	Sometimes his father's jacket. The dressing was weird really because half the laugh was that the clothes didn't fit us, you see. They were all borrowed clothes from our adult people. And Doctor Brown's jacket was like an overcoat more or less, you see, on him, and things like that. But it was all good fun, there was a great laugh about it, and I must say that with us we always got a good reception wi the people, possibly because we did lay on something that our colleagues on the same business, going round the same villages, they didn't do it, you see. They just went in and sang songs and things like that, which we had been doing before my father introduced me to this.
EL	Did you get the impression that the people you were doing it to recognised it?
RH	Some of them did, yes, but not all of them, not necessarily because they were possibly of a younger generation to my father, I don't know. But I never came across it with any-body else of my age group in the village, not even older than us, you see. It just came right from my father and we were – Stenhousemuir and Camelon are not far away, they're only what, a couple of miles? three miles? apart, you know, but they were poles apart people-wise in those days. ... They

	were quite separate. ... We were from Camelon, they were from Stenhousemuir, they were just different, that was the whole thing. ...
EL	How far did you travel, yourself, when you did the play?
RH	Oh, we were only in Camelon, we didn't go any further than that. I mean we were not more than a mile from the house at any time, I don't suppose.
EL	Did you go out just the one night in the year?
RH	Only the one night, Halloween only, that's all. ...
EL	Now you had a little verse you sang at Hogmanay, didn't you? What was that?

RH	That was:
	    Rise up auld wife and shake yer feathers,
	    Dinna think that we are beggars,
	    We are bairns come oot to play,
	    So rise up and gie's our Hogmanay.
	That was in the New Year's morning, we used to go round doing that. ...

EL	So it was New Year's Day you went out?
RH	New Year's Day we'd be out, and that was one rhyme we had, that 'Rise up auld wife and shake your feathers'.
EL	What was the tune of that?
RH	I don't know. We jist recited it. I didn't know any song for it.
EL	So, this is of course different from the *Galatians* now, we're on to Hogmanay and New Year, but which group of children went round together for this New Year thing?
RH	Oh, jist the same ones. I mean we were jist all school chums and we weren't in any groups really. ... On the corner of the place where I lived there were maybe ten to twenty boys of my age, all round about, and we'd be a group of four or five or maybe ten or twelve, it depended, you know, how things went. We were just out playing, you know.
EL	And what time of day did you go?
RH	Oh, that was in the morning about ten, something like that, eight, nine, ten o'clock in the morning until lunchtime.

EL And what did you actually do?

RH Oh, we would often go and just knock at their doors and get an orange or an apple from somebody, that was about all ye got, you know. Nothing very much.

EL So there were several groups of children going round, always on New Year's morning?

RH On New Year's morning, yes, aye. Children weren't out much at night, at least I never knew of any children being out at night on Hogmanay. There was plenty of first-footing went on with teenagers and adults and so on, but nothing else.

EL But Halloween was different? Presumably you went out in the evening?

RH Halloween we were out in the evening. We were out from it got dark at five or six o'clock, and we would be dressed up by that time and away till about half past nine. That was late for us because usually we were in by eight o'clock at night. But Halloween night we were out to about nine-thirty or thereabouts.

EL Did you feel Camelon was a village? ...

RH Aye, it was a village at that time I reckoned. It's all into Falkirk now, of course, and it's grown and grown and grown since then. But as I told you in my letter we're very much conscious of not being the 'Bairns' of Falkirk. They're known as the 'Bairns' in Falkirk. We were the 'Mariners' in Camelon ... supposedly because of Port Downie ... on the Forth and Clyde Canal. ...

EL Did you feel that you could cover the whole village?

RH Well, we wouldn't cover the whole village, it was bigger than that. Also it was in districts, you didn't go certain places because they were rough people there and you didn't go other places because they were well-to-do people, like that, you know. There wis various boundaries that were invisible, but they were there just the same.

EL But you did go to visit people you didn't know?

RH   Oh yes, yes, you just knocked on anybody's door and got in or didn't get in. Sometimes they would chase you or sometimes they would say, 'Come in', you know. Most of the time they did take us in, right enough, we didn't have much trouble that way.

EL   What did you say when you knocked?

RH   Oh, 'Please help the guisers', that was the usual query, you see, and some of them would say, 'Oh, just come in', you know. …

EL   So there'd be five of you together, all dressed up?

RH   Yes.

EL   Did any particular person knock at the door?

RH   Oh, usually me.

EL   Yes, you were the leader.

RH   I probably was, due to the fact that I had been the instigator of the play, but it was my father that put *me* on to it.

EL   So if they let you in, they'd open the door and what would happen?

RH   Oh they'd just say, 'Come in', you see, and then you were into, usually it was just the kitchen, these places were village houses, you know, and we just got started and –

EL   Now, were you all in the kitchen?

RH   Oh, a thing I forgot till just now. Ah, we – I didn't put this in the writing because I had forgotten it, it just come to me now – when we went in, I would turn and say:

> Stir up that fire and make it rattle,
> For in this house there'll be a battle.
> If you don't believe the words I say,
> I'll call in Galatians to clear my way.

I forgot all about that till now when you mentioned that. That was another bit that just came back to me. And that was the opening gambit for it, yes, I forgot about that one. And then Galatians would come in, 'Here comes in Galatians', and go on from there, you see.

EL   Were you in two groups a little bit?

RH   Aye, we used to leave Doctor Brown and Johnny Funny outside in the lobby, they'd hang about in the lobby while there were three of us inside, yeah. That started it off. And then we called in Doctor Brown, of course, after Galatians had been slain and then Johnny Funny came in at the end to collect what we were all going to get in the way of baksheesh, money.

EL   So one of you didn't speak at all, is that right? The one you sent out for Doctor Brown?

RH   Aye, he just hung about and he was sent for Doctor Brown.

EL   How was he dressed?

RH   Oh just dressed up as well. Mostly it was a case of getting into *fancy* dress for the guising ye see. ... Other groups used to be out and a common thing was, not doing plays like *Galatians*, but a common thing was for the boys to get dressed up in girls' clothes and girls getting dressed up in boys' clothes vice versa. But they were the ones that my father reckoned weren't doing very much at all, you see, that they should be doing more than that. And I think that goes on to a great extent even today, though there's not much guising now, today. We've had them here, though, once or twice.

EL   What did wee Johnny Funny collect in? Did he do the collecting?

RH   Aye, he collected whatever pennies they were gonnae give us. We'd usually get thruppence or fourpence from them, sixpence if you were lucky.

EL   From a whole family?

RH   From a family, yes.

EL   How did he collect? With his hands?

RH   Oh, he just had a tin. ... He'd shake it up. ... It was not a tin with a slot in it or anything. ... It was an empty vegetable tin or something like that, a tin can with an open top. ...

EL   Oh well, now, let's think about how the Doctor came in when he was called in by this nameless fellow. How did the Doctor come in?

RH	He just come bustling in as though he was a doctor on his rounds and had been called in for an accident. He would get, sometimes would pull his jacket off and get down to the bloke and go through his motions as to reviving him, you see, but there wasn't much to it. I mean we were never very professional or anything like that and never into – We were wanting to get through with it and get out and into the next house, ye see, we didn't want to spend a lot o time anywhere. So he would do his revival stuff with Galatians and get him back on his feet again.
EL	Oh well, describe that to me, how did he do this revival stuff?
RH	Oh well, it's difficult to say, he would just mutter about and dive in his bag and get his things out, his knives and forks out to make a laugh, you see, and then get his bottle and glass out and go through the motions of pouring a liquid into him. He never that I can remember – I don't think that we ever had any liquid in them, I don't think so. And then he would just pour it round as though it was giving him a drink of some potion to – And then he miraculously wakened up and got on his feet again. That was all really.
EL	Did the Doctor have words? I can't recall now whether you said that or not?
RH	No, I can't remember any words that we had for him.
EL	Sometimes something like, 'In come I Doctor Brown'?
RH	Yes, I believe there is but I can't remember that. I have a notion that there's the line that I had, 'Take a run around the town and see if you can roust up Doctor Brown', but I can remember something about, 'Here comes in Doctor Brown', something about him being the best doctor that was around, but I can't remember the words at all. ... I can't think that it was 'the best doctor in the town' because that was already in the verse where I said, to roust him out in the town, you know? But there was a rhyme with his name, Doctor Brown, but I can't remember it.
EL	Did you ask him, or did anyone ask him, what he could cure?

GALOSHINS REMEMBERED

RH I have a notion that there was a verse about him – I'm making this up now because I can't remember the details – that he had leeches and this and that and the next thing in his bag, but I can't remember it, you know, and I could be kidding myself on it. But it's vaguely in the back of my mind like I remembered that bit about the fireplace, to stir up the fire, just now. I'd forgotten all about that. But I've tried and I can't remember the Brown bit at all.

EL Was there anything about paying the Doctor, that he would be paid so many pounds or anything? How much –

RH There was, but I can't remember any details of it, you know. I believe there was an argument, that he wanted so much for doing that. ... They had an argument about whether he was going to do it or whether he wasn't going to do it, but I can't for the life of me remember it. But I must have known it at the time because the whole thing came from my father. There was nobody else that we knew who did this, you see. ...

Stir Up	Stir up that fire and make it rattle,
	For in this house there'll be a battle.
	If you don't believe the words I say,
	I'll call in Galatians to clear my way.
Galatians	Here comes in Galatians,
	Galatians is my name,
	With sword and pistol by my side
	I hope to win the game.
Stir Up	The game sir, the game sir,
	It's not within your power
	I'll cut you up in slices
	In less than half an hour.
Galatians	You sir?
Stir Up	Yes, me sir.
Galatians	Take out your sword and try, sir.

And then we had the battle.

        Away you go and scout around the town,
        To see if you can roust out Doctor Brown.

And then Doctor Brown would come in and try his medicine on Galatians to revive him and, having revived him, then there was a knock at the door and

Johnny Funny Here comes in wee Johnny Funny,
The man that takes in aa the money.
With long, long pooches doon my knees,
For ha'pennies, pennies and wee bawbees.

But that's as much as I can remember.

EL So he did a knock too?

RH Aye, he knocked on the door and come in. He was in of course, in the lobby, but just standing back, you know.

EL Now this fellow that you sent out to get Doctor Brown, you were saying to me just now that he did a bit of speaking.

RH Aye, but I can't remember what it was, you see. He went off and came back with him. And then Brown had a bit as well, I know that, but I can't remember the details of it. But it was all in doggerel rhyme like that, you know.

EL Do you remember the names of all the boys you did it with?

RH I can remember some of them, Donald Logan and Robert Pagan and Allen, I couldn't remember Allen's first name, he was called Pinnie Allen because his father had a stiff leg from the war, you know. But he was my closest friend right enough, Allen. And another was Boucher, a French name you know. … Alec Young.

EL Did you take the same parts?

RH Usually the same parts each year, you know. … Pinnie Allen, that was his nickname, he used to do Galatians and I did the one that killed him. And Doctor Brown was Donald Logan, Logan was the Doctor. And a boy called Queen, John Queen, was the Johnny Funny, to collect the money.

EL And who was the one you sent out?

RH Oh that was Laidlaw, Tom Laidlaw.

EL I think you've given me more boys' names, have you? Did you have different people in different years?

RH Well, there might have been, you know, there was Pinnie

	Allen, Tom Laidlaw, Donald Logan and John Queen, he was the Johnny Funny. That's only four, isn't it? And myself, that's five.
EL	Then Boucher, did you say?
RH	Boucher, aye. ... I'm not sure he took part in it; he was slightly older than us, he was nine months older, I would think. This was all a crowd that we hung around wi, there were twice as many as that for other things, but at the Halloween I think they were the only ones that took part in it.
EL	When you did other things as groups of boys together, did you divide up the village? Did you have your section of the village?
RH	Oh yeah, we had all gangs, that was the thing, you see. Various small areas had their groups, you know.
EL	Did your area have a name?
RH	No, not really, it was just the particular street.
EL	What was that? ...
RH	That was in Hamilton Street in Camelon. It's just being refurbished now. There were tenement blocks that were built by Hamilton Brown in Glasgow, they were property dealers, you know, and they built these houses for the foundry workers earlier on, before my time. ...
EL	Do you know how many years you went out?
RH	It was all of five, anyway, four or five.
EL	What age did you start?
RH	I would think about when I started ... eight to ten, I should think. That would be in 1923 to '25 I should think, you know, about that time. ... We moved from Camelon to Grahamstown, Falkirk, '27, cos I was twelve then, you see, and I didn't do it after that, no. No, that's up to 1927 was as far as we went, and it probably started about '23. ...
EL	Now some of you had swords, didn't you? How many of you carried swords?
RH	Well, two of us, Galatians and myself, and I think I told you in the letter we made them at school in our woodwork class.

	It was a copy of a Roman backsword, you know, well they called it a backsword. It wasn't really a sword for fencing because the Roman sword was a chopping sword, it wasn't a rapier-type thing. ...
EL	And how did you carry them when you arrived at the house?
RH	We had them in a belt, just stuck in our belt, you see. ...
EL	And how did the two of you fight?
RH	Oh, we just did our fencing stuff, you see, that's it. But the swords themselves were not for fencing really, there's a difference I'm telling you. But that's because we made them at school.
EL	And how long a fight was it, how long did you fight?
RH	Oh just a half-a-minute or a minute, there was nothing to it, just a few passes around here and there. As I say, we were never wanting to stay on anywhere too long. I mean it was a case of getting through with it and getting on to the next one.
EL	You said something about you might vary the length of the fight.
RH	Well that would – depended how it was going in the house, how we were getting on with the people you know. If they were responsive or not, you know.
EL	You would do it if they were responsive?
RH	Aye, we sometimes went through it twice.
EL	What, the fight?
RH	Aye, through the fight twice. I can't remember why. Just come to me now that we did.
EL	And was the Doctor reckoned a comic?
RH	Oh yes, aye, and so wis Johnny Funny, he was a comic as well, you know. Supposed to be anyway.
EL	What exactly did Johnny Funny wear?
RH	Oh he just got dressed up ridiculous really you see. Sometimes – we never used girls' clothes much, others did, but we didn't – oh he'd be dressed up clown-fashion, you know like funny nose and things like that, you know, that sort of stuff and face painted up you know.

EL   A nose actually attached, made out of something?

RH   I think of cardboard, a cardboard nose. I'm just trying to think of it, yes, and his eyes made up clown-fashion right enough with colour, but I can't remember how, not a thing about it, not having been involved in it myself, you know.

EL   You spoke of blackened faces. Who are the blackened faces?

RH   Well, very often we all had them, you know. We got some soot and blackened our faces to go out, you know.

EL   But not Johnny Funny?

RH   No, he was coloured up with other stuff, but can't think what because lipstick wasn't the thing in those days much, you know. I mean it might have been but I don't think so.

EL   The Doctor had a bowler hat. ... Did the rest of you have hats at all?

RH   Oh, we had hats right enough, but they were usually soft hats that we used and we had them pinned up at the side, the highwayman type of thing, an auld soft hat with a pin stuck in the side to hold it up at the side like the Australians' jungle-hat sort of thing. But Doctor Brown invariably had a bowler hat on, you know. We'd to stuff them all wi paper, they were too big for us anyway, you see. We used to put the paper inside the hat band, you know, so as it would fit us.

EL   Did you ever use anything else to blacken your faces besides soot?

RH   No, just the soot. It was easily then done, of course, cos it was all open fires in those days. You just put your hand up the chimney and got some. That was it.

EL   You've got a bit here in your letter about 'our dress was just made up of a sort of cloth smock gathered with a belt'.

RH   Aye, that's right it was a – we got usually some cloths from my mother and old sheets and that, just with a hole cut for your head and hanging over your shoulders and tied round with a rope, you see. There was a belt, usually a belt that was also holding your trousers up on the inside as well. Cos

	we were all in shorts, of course, and this obviously stuck into that, in the belt of that.
EL	So it was shorts, not long trousers, or did you sometimes have long trousers?
RH	Oh, well the likes of Doctor Brown, he had long trousers on, but we – I'm talking about Galatians and myself, we had a sort of smock on you see to – it was a military type of thing, it was supposed to be like the crusaders or something like that, but this was all just made up as we went you see.
EL	It would be white sheet?
RH	It was mostly white, you know, because old sheets that my mother would have, you know, they were all white in those days; there were no coloured sheets.
EL	Did she help you generally with the dressing-up?
RH	Oh, she was pretty good, aye. …
EL	What would you call it, this sheet thing?
RH	Just a shirt really, a smock really, cos she just used to cut a hole in it, it was all old stuff you see and you got your head through that and it wasn't even stitched down the sides. It was just tied round with a string, ye see. [Your arms] were out through the side, no sleeves or anything you know, you'd just wear [an] ordinary jersey or whatever it was you had on, you know, underneath.
EL	That's quite a picture!
RH	And then as I say an old hat of my father's, and he just turned it up at the side and stuck a pin in it to hold it up, military-type, you know.
EL	You say you wore your ordinary shoes and stockings.
RH	Yes, oh yes.
EL	But you mention here a sort of paper helmet that you might wear.
RH	We did that a couple of times, but I can't remember. I think that was done at school as well, again I'm not clear on it though. Mostly it was old soft hats we had, you know, what they call the trilby hat, but there was some helmet we made

one time, I'm trying to think what it was – whether it was at school. It must have been at school we did it cos we had little facilities in the house for doing these things you see. I can't think how it was. I think there was one of those school teachers – when we did the swords he sort of entered into it in a bit you know, in a way, I can't think to what extent he did, and he may have been instrumental in making the helmet, the paper helmet thing at that time. ...

EL So in one house what would they give you for a performance?

RH Och it could be – depending on the number of adults who were there you'd get tuppence or thruppence from each of them, like that. We have had as much as five shillings in a night which was quite something in those days.

EL Was that five shillings for the group?

RH Between us, aye for the group, oh yes, aye.

EL How did you divide up the money?

RH Well we just split it equally, I mean that was it. Split it in five.

EL Did Johnny Funny carry it about?

RH Aye, he carried it about, but of course outside there was a post mortem straight away to see how much we had got, you know. Whether we had got thruppence or sixpence or whatever, you know. But a thrupenny bit was quite common, or a sixpence or pennies you know. If there were three or four adults there, you'd maybe get tuppence from each of them or something like that.

EL And what else did you get?

RH Sometimes you got a bit of cake and a drink o lemonade or something like that you know, but that was beside the point, you know.

EL Were you given fruit?

RH Not a lot, but ... well apples and nuts of course were quite common you know cos we always had dooking for apples at Halloween, you know, and nuts.

EL What sort of nuts, any special sort?

RH No, nearly all hazelnuts mostly.

EL   Did you go collecting nuts yourself?
RH   I have done all my days, actually, I still collect them. ...
     But we used to have in the house, before we'd ever go out
     on this, we'd have dooking for apples, you know, and the
     Halloween business swirling them round in the bath, you
     know. ... My father was a great boy for getting you all dookt
     in the bath! Because he wouldna let you get your hands in,
     you know. There would be a tin bath in the middle o the
     floor and we'd have a go at that, you see, swirl the apples
     round about and then you'd to get them out with your teeth
     or you didn't get them at all, you know.

13 *James Wands – Dennyloanhead, 1912–1916*

Mr Wands wrote to me in response to the appeal for information in *The Scots Magazine* of January 1982 and I recorded him, along with Catherine Nickolls, at his home in Denny, Stirlingshire, on 12 March 1982 (SA1982.110) when he was aged 79. His date of birth was 12 December 1902. When he performed in the play as a boy he lived at Dennyloanhead which is nine miles south of Stirling and four miles to the west of Camelon where Robert Hendry acted [12]. Mr Wands spoke and sang the play again after the performance noted here, and in the second text Goshen says: 'Oh my, what have I done?' and 'What about my friend Jock here? What can you do for him?'. The Doctor in this second text says: 'I can cure all sorts, anything from lumbago to heartache and backache and bellyache' and 'Oh, someone comes'. In a text written out by Mr Wands, the Doctor on entering adds 'and with my bag I'm always on call' after 'town'. He says simply 'Anything and anybody' when he is asked what he can cure, and, after the cure, says, 'Rise up Jock'. According to a note included in the correspondence, Johnny Funny wore trousers down past his knees 'with pockets stitched on to his knees'. Mr Wands wrote about recalling 'many happy times' taking part in the play and his enjoyment was evident throughout the recording session which gave us 'many a good laugh', just as he had remembered the play doing in the past.

EL   What about this play you used to do at Halloween?
JW   Oh, the 'Stir Up Your Fire'?
EL   Yes.
JW   Oh, it was good – play aa the different parts. Used to go roun aa the houses. I mind one time we went into the hotel at Dennyloanhead and I was Stir Up that night and I gaes in wi a wee sword about this size, a toy sword:

> Stir up your fire and give us light
> For in this house there'll be a fight.
> If you don't believe a word I say
> I'll call upon Jock Slasher.

And just wi that the hotel owner just bent down the back o the bar and drew out a great big sword that size, and of course I, out the door! But eh, I got chased back in again and then we carried on wi our show and it was the best night ever we had for collection, in the bar o the hotel, you see.

EL   Do you remember how much you got?
JW   Oh no, I couldnae mind that. Oh no, if ye got a penny you were doing well in these days, that was afore the First World War.
CN   Did they give you other things?
JW   No, that was, at that time we jist got the money.
CN   They didn't give you nuts –?
JW   No, nothing like that, no at Halloween. It was Halloween we aye played, ye see. Oh no, they was needing all their nuts and apples for their own families I think.
EL   How many houses would you go round in a night usually?
JW   Oh, I couldnae jist tell you that. There's be – aa that terrace would be twelve, fourteen – I think we'd dae about thirty to

	forty houses in a night. [EL: Really!] Start at half-past five and finish about ten o'clock
EL	Oh, you did a good evening's work!
JW	Oh, we did, yes!
EL	You did the whole play every time?
JW	Every time and we sung a song, a chorus of some kind. What was the – 'Horo my nut brown maiden' was our favourite, that was our favourite, it was easy sung.
EL	Do you still sing?
JW	No me, I couldna sing.
EL	There was no singing in the play itself? This was a separate song?
JW	Aye, after we finished, usually after the collection came in, after Wee Johnnie Funny came in. Ah well, Stir Up and Jock Slasher they sung, 'Here's two warriors going to fight', they sung that bit.
EL	Oh, they did?
JW	Aye. 'These two warriors going to fight wha've never fought before' and Goshen he carries on, 'I'll give anyone a hundred pounds to put Jock Slasher to the floor'. And then after Doctor Brown comes in and cures Jock Slasher – it was usually sugarallie water we had – you know sugarallie water – he tells him to rise up and Jock Slasher, he sings:

> Once I was dead but now I am alive,
> Blessed be the Doctor that made me alive.
> We'll all join hands and never fight no more,
> We'll be as good a friends as we've ever been
>   before.

EL	And how does the tune go? You've probably got it in your mind.
JW	Aye, just what I was singing the now, not much o a tune.
EL	A wee bit more of a tune, maybe? A wee bit more of a tune, was there?
JW	A wee bit more, uh huh.
EL	How did it go, do you think?

JW Oh

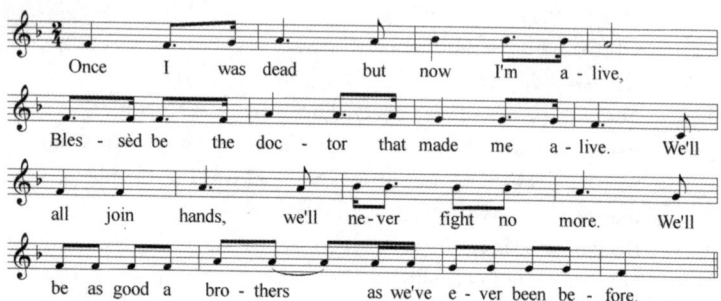

Once I was dead but now I'm a-live,
Bles-sèd be the doc-tor that made me a-live. We'll
all join hands, we'll ne-ver fight no more. We'll
be as good a bro-thers as we've e-ver been be-fore.

EL Oh, that's great!

JW And then Doctor Brown cures Jock, tells him – oh he sung that after he cured him. And then somebody says, 'Oh someone comin'', and in comes Wee Johnnie Funny, aa dressed up:

> Here comes in Wee Johnnie Funny.
> The best wee man tae gaither the money.
> Long leather pooches doon tae his knees.
> A penny or tuppence or three bawbees.

That was yer collection and then sometimes we sung a song then, ye see?

EL Yes, that was the free choice? Did they sometimes ask you for something special?

JW No, no, they just took us for granted in these days. Nowadays ye cannae get them to dae anything.

EL So how many of you went out doing it?

JW Four, just the four.

EL So the characters, who were –?

JW Goshen – we called him Goshen ye see – Jock Slasher, Doctor Brown and Johnnie Funny, four. See that made it just nice four, ye see. Any more and ye would be short of cash when it came to count it up!

EL Who was the first one that spoke?

JW Goshen.

EL He has the first line?

JW	He comes in, 'Stir up yer fire', aye, we just, when ye asked anyone tae play it, 'Would ye be Stir Up?' You know we didnae say, 'Will you be Goshen?'. 'Will you play Stir Up?'
EL	Ah, that was the same man that you call Stir Up or Goshen?
JW	Stir Up, Goshen, aye. Och aye, we did aa the parts back in – well I never played Johnnie Funny, I was either Jock Slasher or Stir Up.
CN	Would you exchange parts during the evening?
JW	Sometimes. It depends what house ye went tae. If ye went tae your friend's, you were Stir Up, you see?
EL	Was that the most important?
JW	That was the most important yin. Because if you went in – you jist walked into the house ye know, no chapping, knocking at the door in these days – opened the door and 'Stir up yer fire!', ye see? Well, ye always went in when it was yer friend's, ye see, you didnae get chased.
EL	Oh, I see, it was the first who went in –
JW	Very rarely we got chased, very rarely. Oh I could hardly – I would say we never really got chased.
EL	They always let you finish?
JW	They always let us in and finish the show. Suppose you only got a copper, it was aye something.
EL	I wonder, would you do the words right through from the beginning to the end, just the actual words of the play? And sing the bits that were sung?
JW	I'll try it.
EL	That would be grand.

JW *Goshen*   Stir up yer fire and give us light,
For in this house there'll be a fight.
If you don't believe a word I say,
I'll call upon Jock Slasher.

Jock Slasher   Here comes in Jock Slasher,
Jock Slasher is my name.
Sword and pistol by my side,
I hope to win the game.

Goshen	The game sir, the game sir,
	Is not within your power.
	I'll slice you down in inches
	In less than half an hour.
Jock Slasher	You sir?
Goshen	Yes, me sir.
Jock Slasher	Draw out your sword and try.

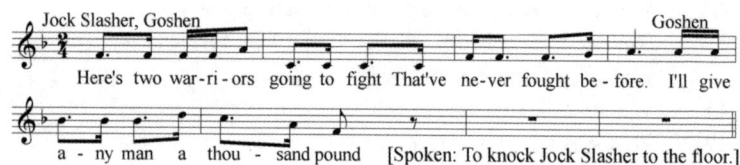

Goshen	Ah, what have I done? Have I killed my old friend, Jock Slasher. Ah, I know, I'll send for old Doctor Brown.
Doctor Brown	Here comes in old Doctor Brown, The best old doctor in the town.
Goshen	What can you cure?
Doctor Brown	I can cure all sorts, anything from rheumatics to lumbago or anything you like.
Goshen	Well what about my friend, Jock?

Doctor Brown goes over and gives him the sugarallie water.

| *Doctor Brown* | Rise up old man and give us a song! |

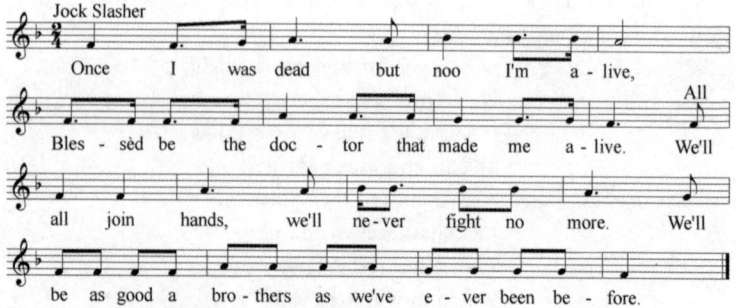

Doctor Brown	Ah, someone else is comin.
Johnnie Funny	Here comes in Wee Johnnie Funny,
	The best wee man tae gaither the money.
	Long leather pooches doon tae his knees,
	A penny, or tuppence, or three bawbees.

EL   That's great.

JW   That's it!

EL   Did someone say, 'Someone else is coming'?

JW   Aye, Doctor Brown usually said it when it's Johnnie Funny.

EL   And did he knock at the door?

JW   No, he just came in too. You just came in in these days onyway.

EL   And this was in Dennyloanhead?

JW   Aye.

EL   How many nights did you go out?

JW   We just went out the one night.

EL   So you worked hard that one evening!

JW   Aye, the night before Halloween.

EL   Before Halloween, or Halloween itself?

JW   Sometimes Halloween, but it was usually the night before.

EL   Oh, and what did you do on Halloween itself?

JW   Well, we maybe had our own parties you see. But sometimes we went out on Halloween night, it depends.

EL   But only once.

JW   Only once, oh no, only once. Only one night.

EL   And was there only one group of boys going round the village?

JW   Oh no there were two or three groups, two or three groups. That's the way ye always selected somebody who'd a lot of friends – so you'd get *their* houses. The earlier ye went the better, ye see? But ye see it was a long village, well ye had a good – there was Dennyloanhead and then there was Parkfoot and then Longcroft. Well, we did a bit of Dennyloanhead and all Parkfoot, that was our – we never went away up to – sometimes we went away up to Longcroft if

	there was a laddie in the four that had friends up there. That's the only time we went up that way; ye always went where there were friends of the cast.
EL	Well, you've got a wonderful memory of it. How many years did you go out, do you think?
JW	Oh well, before the war and just during the war tae, we'd be about fourteen, we didnae go after we were fourteen.
EL	What age did you start?
JW	Oh about nine year old, nine or ten. Aye, I'd be nine or ten when we started.
EL	Do you remember the names of the boys you went out with? Is that too much to ask?
JW	Oh, oh. There was Jim Stark, Hendry Boyd, Crawford Boyd, Robert Black, I don't know, some ither yins. Will Gibb – maybe an odd yin different times. Ye always went with yer pal, yer pal at the time, that year.
EL	You'd know them at school, of course, you were all at school together?
JW	Oh aye. … You always had four, you couldnae play the thing without the four. Oh ye'd plenty offers, 'Will we get in your team this year?' sorta style.
EL	And you decided on the ones that had the most friends that would bring in the money?
JW	That was the idea.
CN	Where did you learn it from? Who taught it to you?
JW	I think it must've been older boys that told me but I can't remember about that, it must've been older boys.
EL	The first time you went out were you the youngest of the group, do you think?
JW	No, there was two of us about the same age. In fact we're both our ages in December. We'd be about the same. We would be the youngest, us two, for tae start wi like.
EL	So who was that, your close friend, then?
JW	Robert Black. …
EL	And how did you get dressed up when you did the play?

JW	Oh you just got anything that was fancy at aa. Stir Up Goshen usually try and get a big hat with a big feather, some kind of a hat. We usually had an old boy-scout hat or wan o these big fancy ladies' hats, straw, ye could pit a feather in. And any fancy – a kinda blouse or something, and pit a sash roon aboot it and yer sword, yer wooden sword through yer sash. It didnae matter for yer trousers or anything like that as long as ye had something fancy on round there, and maybe a cravat, a home-made cravat. Then Jock Slasher, he would be much the same but we usually tried to get an old soldier's jacket. We carried a red one for a long while, ken, a red old soldier's jacket, red, and his belt and his sword and pistol and his big feather, always had a feather in their hats somehow. Doctor Brown he came in with a trilby or a bowler hat and his coat and his wee brown bag. Well I had a Gladstone bag, an old Gladstone bag. That was the typical doctor's bag in these days and it belonged to my father, so I always got the use of that. And then Wee Johnnie Funny he made up his own rig-oot wi' his big bunnet, skip away tae the side and a big long scarf hingin like Oor Wullie, you know? Something like Oor Wullie. And his artificial pockets away down. Long trousers he had always on.
EL	Oh well tell us about the pockets.
JW	They were just made, right in front o there, just great big pockets stitched on to an old pair o trousers. This was the idea, long leather pooches. It wis sometimes jist a bit ordinary-like cloth, and that was Johnnie Funny. ... He put his hands in, coming in, walking in, 'Long leather pooches doon tae ma knees'.
EL	Did he walk a special sort of way?
JW	Aye, well he usually come in wi his hands in his pockets, to let them know, drawing attention tae his long leather pooches.
EL	What did he have on the upper part of him?
JW	Oh he'd on onything, I've seen us, we'd jerseys for two or three years, auld football jerseys, that's what he had on.

EL	And what would you have on your feet?
JW	Oh just your ordinary footwear.
CN	Did you disguise your faces?
JW	Sometimes we made moustaches, Jock Slasher and Goshen painted a 'stache; some o them painted a wee beard.
EL	How did you paint it?
JW	Oh just wi burnt cork, just wi burnt cork.
EL	So you didn't blacken the rest of your faces, just the moustache and the wee beard?
JW	Oh no, no, because if you blackened your face you'd maybe no get in some o the houses where there were kids, you see.
EL	Why that?
JW	Well, the kids'd maybe get a frighten wi black faces ye see.
EL	So did you say it was just Goshen and Jack Slasher that would have their faces done?
JW	Well sometimes Doctor Brown, depends who we had. If you got somebody to put a false moustache on him.
EL	Would it be black, for the Doctor.
JW	Naw, it was usually a grey, ken, no black, but you know, a kinda grey moustache.
EL	He'd be an older man?
JW	He was usually kinda looked older, tried to be made up older, you know what I mean.
EL	Did you do anything special to his hair?
JW	Naw, well, he'd always his hat on, you see, he kept it on aa the time.
EL	So how much money do you think you'd make in a night?
JW	Ach well, about, we got about, let me see. I'd say about one and tuppence each. If we got about five bob for a night we were doing well. A penny was a penny in these days.
EL	How did you divide it up amongst you?
JW	Well, after we were finished we divided it in four.
EL	And Wee Johnnie, of course, had it all.
JW	He had it aa in his pockets.
EL	Did he divide it up, do you think?

JW	Well, whoever was captain of the team divided it.
EL	And who was captain?
JW	Whae-ever started that team. Maybe somebody would come to me and, 'Are ye gaun oot guising, are ye fixed up?' 'No.' 'Well, come wi us.' Some of your pals, like. That's how we did it.
EL	I expect you've been captain once or twice?
JW	Och aye. ...
EL	Did [the doctor] take things out of the bag? Did he open the bag?
JW	He would usually have a wee bottle or something and it was usually sugarallie water, you know what sugarallie is?
EL	Perhaps you'd better tell us.
JW	It was sugarallie, it's a black stick and you just put it in a bottle and let it melt and it turns black. And we were under the delusion that if you put it below the bed it went blacker quicker! We used to do that thinking it was going blacker quicker! And that was his medicine, you see?
CN	What did it taste like? Was it sweet?
JW	Oh it was quite sweet. Jock Slasher got a drink of it.
EL	So Goshen killed –
JW	Jock Slasher and Doctor Brown brought him back to life.
EL	And he had a wee bottle in his bag?
JW	We always had it, he opened his bag, oh yes. You had to do that job. And of course the folks were wondering what was coming out the wee bag, it kept them guessing.
EL	Do you think the Doctor maybe, if he was among his friends, did he say a bit more?
JW	Oh he elaborated, depends on who it was. He'd add what he'd like to the show.
EL	Was he a funny fellow, was he a comic?
JW	Usually was a bit of a comic.
EL	You've done that part too, have you?
JW	I've done that part too, yes. ...
CN	When do you think people stopped doing it?

JW Ah, well, I think the First World War. I don't remember anybody, kids, coming after the First World War. See the War chynged an awful lot, so it did, First World War. I've never seen anybody after us. See, we were just the age when the war started.

EL So you think maybe you're the last ... ?

JW I think we were about the last that I know of, maybe no, but I think we were. ...

EL Did you do anything special at New Year as well?

JW Naw, we jist ... no, we didnae. We always jist went out at Halloween and that sort of thing anyway. Oh no, you couldnae go too often tae folks in these days. A copper was a copper! ...

EL When the doctor's curing [Jock Slasher], what does he actually do with the sugarallie water?

JW Oh he goes down and lifts up his head and gives him the bottle, a drink out o his bottle.

EL Ah, he gives him a wee drink, he puts it in his mouth?

JW Puts it in his mouth – oh he got drinks o it, there's no doot about that! I've seen the bottle empty before we were halfway through! Anyway, that's what he does, and Jock, he kinda sits up. By that time he's putting his bottle in his bag and he tells him to rise up.

EL And when you're singing all together at the end, how were you all standing?

JW Well, we're just standing, the four of us, in a half-circle. That's what we usually did.

EL Facing which way?

JW Well, maybe at the door facing the audience or the people in the house.

EL Did you take hands at all?

JW Well we all joined hands, the three of us when it was 'all join hands', you see. But when Johnnie Funny comes in, that was different.

EL Oh, I see, before Johnnie Funny comes in –

JW	The three of us are standing with our hands, joined our hands.
EL	In a circle?
JW	In a circle.
EL	A complete circle?
JW	Ah, well, you know, if three can make a circle.
EL	Yes, that's interesting. And then at the end you just –
JW	Just all lined up.
EL	And did the audience put the money in Johnnie Funny's pockets, or did they give it into his hand?
JW	Oh, they give it into his hand. Jist went round and held out his hand, more or less. Och, aye, you never got a refusal anyway, in these days, supposing it was only a copper.
EL	From a whole household?
JW	Ah, well if there was younger yins working, you know, some of them working, you aye got about – I think the best ever we got was tenpence, that I remember, in the hotel bar, that night we got chased oot and brought back again.
EL	What did the minister think of all this? Did you go to the manse?
JW	Oh, oor manse was away up at Longcroft, the church I went to, you see.
EL	Out of your beat.
JW	It was out of our beat.
EL	Did you call it a beat? I'm putting words into your mouth!
JW	We'd have got chased – we'd have got chased if we'd have went up that length.
EL	Oh, what happened?
JW	Every crowd had their own district, you see. We never – Dennyloanhead we went to the corner, what we caad it, it wis the road to Falkirk and Stirling, that was whit – we didnae get any further than that. Well the hotel was there, we got playing in there, but we never got playing further up.
EL	Did you ever try?

JW Naw, there were aye somebody there, you see. Ye didnae want tae encroach, as it were.

EL Do you think there would have been a fight?

JW Ach, I don't think so.

EL But you just knew?

JW You just knew to keep out their territory. I'll put it that way, territory.

EL Would there be several groups on the upper bit, and the other bits?

JW Oh, aye, there were always groups an that, and I don't know if they, the lower part of the village played the same as us. But I think they would, cos sometimes we had a lad fae the lower part, when I got a chance at him, Doctor Brown. He was stocky built, he wore his father's hat and his auld swallow-tail coat. Oh, he was a toff!

EL He was your best Doctor Brown, was he?

JW Oh, quite easy.

EL What was his name?

JW Will Gibb. A pal of mines, he died there about three year ago. We were pals for years after, in later years when we played football together. Pals for years. Oh, he was a born comic, him.

EL Did you go straight from school into the foundry?

JW Oh, yes, aye. I was fourteen in December and I was working in January, after the New Year holidays.

EL So you did the play while you were still schoolboys, but when you started work you –?

JW Just schoolboys – oh, we didnae – When the War started, we played it during the War, up tae we were age tae go tae work, and then we didnae play after.

14 Andrew Rennie – Kippen, 1899–1903

The village of Kippen lies ten miles west of Stirling. In Australia, I had recorded a memory of *Galoshins* from Mrs Margaret Shepherd (*née* Clark) who came from Kippen (SA1977.023) and she told me that the village blacksmith, Andrew Rennie, was a mine of information. And so he was! When I proposed visiting Kippen to explore its possibilities for the play with three students from Stirling University – Karin Harrington, Tracey Heaton and Rob Watling – Rob enquired ahead and was put onto Mr Rennie and arranged a meeting. We met Mr Rennie in his smithy on 15 November 1979 and he launched straight into a performance when we asked what he did at Hogmanay (SA1979.173). He had taken the part of the presenter, Keep Silence. He was in his ninetieth year at this time, he told us, but he was still full of vigour. The play had meant a great deal to him and he was delighted to be associated with our activities. Tracey did a dissertation on his work as a blacksmith, while Rob produced a hand-printed booklet, *Two Stirlingshire Hero-Combat Plays*, which includes the Rennie version and the similar one published by James Maidment in 1835 (Hayward, 280–84). In 1981 we arranged for a video to be made at the University of Stirling that first shows Mr Rennie performing the play and being interviewed by Tracey about it, and then shows a performance of *Galoshins* by five boys from Kippen Primary School who had been specially taught the play by Mr Rennie (see illustrations). Mr Rennie performed the play very similarly on a number of occasions; the version here is from the video recording. The only point where he was hesitant in his text was the single line which he often omitted, but gave once as 'What do you do to cure a dead man?' (SA1979.150B). The video wording given here, 'What do you take to cure a dead man?', indicates that this line is a reminiscence of the bargaining, which starts in the Maidment text with the question 'What will you take to cure this dead man?', to which the Doctor responds, 'Ten pounds and a bottle of wine'.

It was especially remarkable that Mr Rennie knew a sung form of the play and his version allows us to interpret earlier references to sung performances (Hayward, 49, 191, 100–5). The other recorded versions confine the singing to the revival and blessing at the end, apart from the one from James Wands [13], which has the four lines beginning 'Here's two warriors going to fight' as a sung section, and the rather fragmentary one recorded by Hamish Henderson from Mrs Mason in Prestonpans (Hayward, 264–65). I give some extracts from our interviews with Mr Rennie – (a) November 1979, (b) December 1979, (c) video, 1981 – and close with his play text, which is the longest one that has been recorded, although some considerably longer versions are known from print.

RW   What did you wear yourself when you went round guising?
AR   Oh, your faces were all blackened, for a start. And if ye'd any old clothes at all, you put them on, ye see. And then ye'd turn yer jacket sleeves outside in, and the white lining showing, ye see. (b)

KH   And what did you use to blacken your face with?
AR   Soot. There's plenty soot here [in the smithy].
EL   It was a job getting it off afterwards, was it?
AR   Aye! ... We only had *Galoshins* once a year, between Christmas and New Year.
EL   Did you look forward to it?
AR   Oh aye, aye
RW   How many nights did you do it?
AR   Oh well you started at Christmas, did it all to New Year, Hogmanay. That was a week, a full week. (a)

TH   How old would you be when you started to do the play?
AR   Oh, maybe about nine.
TH   And when would you go on through until?
AR   Till you were finished wi the school.

TH   Which would be at?

AR   Fourteen.

TH   Fourteen, because you started apprenticeship as a blacksmith at fourteen, didn't you? So why did you stop when you started work?

AR   Oh, you were too big to go away and guise when you was working!

TH   Oh, I see. Too grown up.

AR   Yes. ...

TH   What was the most important thing about the performance, would you say?

AR   Well, you'd always to be cheerful and happy, you know, and that sort of thing, and aye to make your audience happy too. (c)

AR   It was always before seven just when you knew the workmen would be home and we stopped always about nine, no much after that – two hours. ...

TH   They expected you coming at that time of year. ... If there was a knock at the door they would think, 'Oh that must be the *Galoshins*!'

AR   Yes, especially if they heard voices. You were always blethering and talking and laughing – if they heard that they knew who it was. (c)

AR   It wis a kitchen, jist an old-fashioned kitchen, ye see, an some of the old chairs and tables in it, and you had a family sittin round the kitchen, ye see, maybe two or three kids. And then a rattling wid come tae the door, an ye'd go tae the door an, 'Do ye want *Galoshins*?' And then ye'd say, 'Oh aye, jist come in', ye see, an ye could have aa that in the kitchen. And then this, when the Galoshins an the Admiral start fighting, it's a great thing it, ye see. It was a good fight, ye know, wi swords, ye see, an this sort o thing. ...

RW   And who knocked on the door then?

AR Oh, Keep Silence. He was the boss, ye see. He knocked on the door. ...

RW So, how many people would be watching you usually? The whole family?

AR The whole family, aye. They might have visitors, but they wis usually jist themselves and their children. (b)

EL Did one special person collect the things when you went round?

AR Well, you'd wee Keekem Funny; he'd collect it usually. Often we'd no Keekem Funny. I'd just collect the money. (a)

EL Did the Doctor dress up in something special?

AR Oh, just an old coat on, and this wee bottle he took out his pocket.

TH He didn't have a bag?

AR No, he hadnae a bag.

RW Was there anything in the bottle at all?

AR Water, just. [And the Doctor would] hae on an old hat usually. ... If he could get an old tile hat, that'd be all the better. (a and b)

TH Did you do any rehearsals?

AR Oh, well, we did maybe one or two, but no very many, cos we all knew it off by heart. It was the actions we were doing [at] the rehearsals.

TH Because the actions are quite important, aren't they?

AR Ye see, that fight, ye could make a noise, make a good thing o that, ye see. ...

RW So, how long might the fight last?

AR Well, ye could make the fight last for aboot five minutes, if ye liked. (b)

TH	What did you make the swords out of?
AR	A lath. We cut a bit off for the cross, ye see, and that gave the lath about the right length of sword.
TH	And the lath is something that you'd plaster over, isn't it, in a wall? So it's just like a thin piece of wood.
AR	Aye, about an inch broad, ye see.
TH	And where would you get that from?
AR	We got it from the plasterer's yard. (c)
TH	And was there more than one group of boys that went around?
AR	There was, aye. Maybe about four different gangs.
TH	So what would happen if you ever came across another gang?
AR	There might have been a free fight! … Rivals, you know!
TH	So did you try and avoid each other?
AR	Oh yes. If we seen them coming we'd maybe go another round, ye see. (c)
EL	Did you go all round the village?
AR	Aye, and out to the outlying houses. If you got a good farm house that was the best place. …
RW	And if you went to a house where [another gang] had been, would they still let you in to do your play?
AR	Oh aye, take you in and see wha's the best. (a)
EL	Do you think your father's generation did this play? You didn't learn it from your father?
AR	No, no. No. Ah don't know where we picked it up, it wis jist, it wis well known among the kids at that time.
RW	And did they all do it in exactly the same way?
AR	Aye.
KH	You all had exactly the same words as well?
AR	Yes. Exactly the same words. (b)

GALOSHINS REMEMBERED

Admiral	The game sir, the game sir,
	It's not within yer power,
	I'll slay you down in inches
	In less than half an hour.
Galoshins	You, sir?
Admiral	I, sir.
Galoshins	Take out yer sword and try, sir.

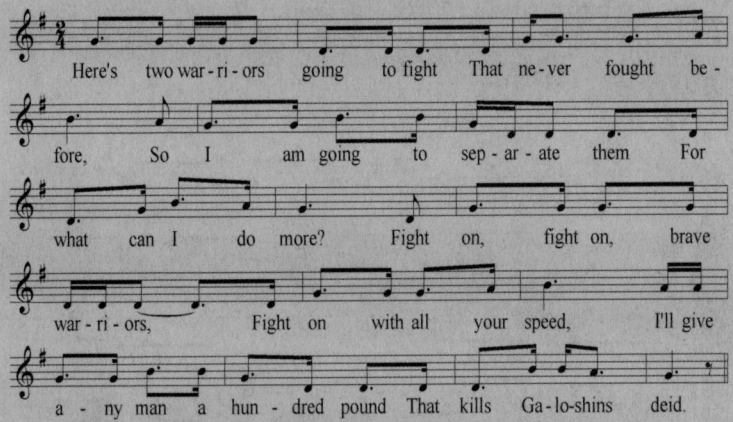

Here's two war-ri-ors going to fight That ne-ver fought be-fore, So I am going to sep-ar-ate them For what can I do more? Fight on, fight on, brave war-ri-ors, Fight on with all your speed, I'll give a-ny man a hun-dred pound That kills Ga-lo-shins deid.

Keep Silence	Around the kitchen, around the hall,
	Old greasy doctor do I call.
Doctor Brown	Here comes in old Doctor Brown,
	The best old doctor in the town,
	A[t] Heeshyspeeshy I learned my trade,
	I came to Scotland to cure the dead.
Keep Silence	What can you cure?
Doctor Brown	All sorts of diseases to be sure.
Keep Silence	What do you take to cure a dead man?
Doctor Brown	I've a little bottle in my waistcoat pocket
	I got from my Aunty Betty when I was
	nine years of age.

GALOSHINS REMEMBERED

A drop on the nose, a drop on the chin,
Get up, old Jack, and sing.

Galoshins

Once I was dead but now I'm alive And blessed be the doctor that made me alive. *All* We'll all join hands an we'll never fight no more, We'll be as good as brothers as we ever were before. We'll bless the master of the house, and bless the mistress too, And all the little babies around the table too. With their pockets full of money and their bottles full of beer, We wish you all a good Hogmanay and a happy New Year.

Keekem Funny   Here comes in wee Keekem Funny,
A'm the man that lifts the money.
If ye've anything to spare,
Jist pop it in there.

NOTES

1. See Lyle, 1988.
2. Hayward, 2007.
3. SA1982.126.
4. SA1979.151.
5. Lyle, 2007.
6. SA1981.091.
7. Macleod Banks, 1.11–13, 40–1, 2.116–7, 165–6; Miller, 1857, 417.
8. Martin, 2007.
9. SA1982.113.
10. cf. Hayward, 92, 128.
11. SA1982.110B.
12. cf. Hayward, 285.
13. SA1982.113.
14. Tom Ovens, SA1984.033B.
15. SA1979.151.
16. SA1984.032A; cf. SA1984.033A.
17. VD008.
18. Hayward, 24–8.
19. cf. the version from Inkerman, Hayward, 207–12.
20. cf. Hayward, 51, 61–62.
21. SA1982.113.
22. SA 1981.091.
23. cf. Hayward, 106.
24. Hayward, 72–84.
25. SA1981.091.
26. William Walker, letter 1982.
27. SA1982.112A.
28. SA1998.100.
29. SA1982.110A.
30. Robb, 19; Hayward, 254–55.
31. SA1980.101A.
32. Smith letters, 4.11.1980, 20.11.1980; cf. Hayward, 287–88, from the Peter T. Millington Collection.
33. SA1979.151.
34. SA1980.091.
35. SA1980.101.

BIBLIOGRAPHY

Anderson, J. M. The Galoshuns and the Guisers, *The Edinburgh Tatler*, v. 23, no. 177 (January 1976), 22.

Cawte, E. C., Helm, A. and Peacock, N. *English Ritual Drama: A Geographical Index*, London, 1967.

Dale, W. The Guisers, *The Falkirk Mail: Our Christmas Annual* (December 1925), 81.

Fergus, D. 'Here Comes in Goloshans', *The Scots Magazine* (January 1982), 420–4, with unascribed and untitled follow-up piece in *The Scots Magazine* (August 1982), 534–35.

Hayward, B. *Galoshins: The Scottish Folk Play*, Edinburgh, 1992.

Hayward, B. The Seasonal Folk Drama Galoshins in Southern Scotland. In Beech, J., Hand, O., MacDonald, F., Mulhern, M. A. and Weston, J., eds. *Oral Literature and Performance Culture* (Scottish Life and Society: A Compendium of Scottish Ethnology, 10), Edinburgh, 2007, 556–70.

Lyle, E. with Bruford, A. The Goloshans, *Tocher*, vol. 5 (no. 32), 1976–82, 107–12.

Lyle, E. with Bruford, A. Galoshins: A New Year Play from Kippen, *Tocher*, vol. 5 (nos 36–37), 1982, 380–83.

Lyle, E. Letter to the Editor headed 'Guiser Play', *The Scots Magazine* (April 1982), 210–12.

Lyle, E. Some Reminiscences of Scottish Traditional Drama, *Traditional Drama Studies* 2, (1988), 19–29.

Lyle, E. *Galoshins*: The Scottish Death-and-Revival Play Performed by Boys at Yule or Hallowe'en. In Gunnell, T., ed. *Masks and Mumming in the Nordic Area*, Uppsala, 2007, 733–41.

Macleod Banks, M. *British Calendar Customs: Scotland*, 3 vols, London, 1937.

Martin, N. A. Game of Two Halves: Guising and Contest in Scotland. In Buckley, A. D., Mac Cárthaigh, C., Ó Cathain, S. and Mac Mathúna, S., eds, *Border-Crossing: Mumming in Cross-Border and Cross-Community Contexts*. Proceedings of a conference held at the Academy of Irish Cultural Heritages,

University of Ulster, Derry, 9–13 June 2003, Dundalk, 2007, 171–201.
Miller, H. *Scenes and Legends of the North of Scotland*, Edinburgh, 1857.
Ramage, W. A. *An Auld Herd's Memories*, n.p., 1983.
Robb, I. F., ed. *Our Village: Newtown St Boswells*, Galashiels, 1966.
Romanosky, L. Hallowe'en in Scotland Past and Present, unpublished MLitt. thesis, University of Edinburgh, 1997.
Trotter, Mrs Senga, Second letter to the Editor under heading 'Goloshons – In Bowden – And Elsewhere', *The Scots Magazine*, (March 1982), 684, 686.
Watling, R., ed. *Two Stirlingshire Hero-Combat Plays*, Stirling, 1980.

Manuscript letters

Anderson, John M., Falkirk
    28.3.1977, to Paul Smith.
    13.11.1980, to EL
Cockburn, Mrs Margaret Cockburn, Innerleithen
    10.3.1982, to EL
Hendry, Robert D., Upper Largo
    25.1.1982, to EL
    Undated reply to letter of 4.2.1982, to EL
Kerr, David, Armadale
    17.7.1993, to EL
Knox, W., Hawick
    Undated letter to David Fergus, forwarded 13.3.1982
Leishman, James H., Wick
    8.5.1982, to EL
Orr, Aileen, Edinburgh
    21.5.1982, to EL
Pratt, Mrs Anne (*née* Smith), Nottingham
    18.11.1980, to EL
Sanderson, Elizabeth M. C., Edinburgh
    12.5.1982, to EL
Smith, Mrs Agnes (*née* Hardie), Nottingham

4.11.1980, to EL
20.11.1980, to EL
Walker, William, Glasgow
Undated, received by 12.5.1982, to Editor of *The Scots Magazine*
Wands, James. M, Denny
Undated response to Fergus article of 1.1982, to Editor of *The Scots Magazine*
19.2.1982, to EL
Williamson, Mrs M.
Undated response to Fergus article of 1.1982, received by 4.2.1982, to EL
Postmarked 26.5.1982, to EL

Recorded sources

Sound recordings (SA) and video recordings (VD) in the Archives of the School of Scottish Studies drawn upon in this book

SA1977.023 Mrs Margaret Shepherd, *née* Clark, EL.
SA1977.205 Wat Ramage, 24.8.1977, EL; James Purves, EL; William Brown with Mrs Nairn, *née* Todd, EL.
SA1979.091 William Brown, Wat Ramage, EL.
SA1979.150 Andrew Rennie, EL with Karin Harrington, Tracey Heaton and Rob Watling.
SA1979.151 Mrs Mollie Strang, *née* Simpson, and Elsie Boag, EL with Karin Harrington, Tracey Heaton and Rob Watling.
SA1979.173, Andrew Rennie, EL with Karin Harrington, Tracey Heaton and Rob Watling.
SA1980.100 John Anderson, EL.
SA1980.101 Isobel Robb, William Bruce, EL.
SA1981.091 Jim MacQueen with his wife Ina, *née* Strang, and her sister, Mrs Isobel Jenkins, EL with Catherine Nickolls and Gordon McCullough.
SA1982.110 James Wands, John Simpson, EL with Catherine Nickolls.
SA1982.113 William Hay, EL.
SA1982.112 John MacFadyen, EL.
SA1982.114 Robert Hendry, EL.

SA1982.115, 116, 117 David Laurie and Mrs Margaret Muir (*née* Laurie), EL.
SA1982.124A Brian Lambie, EL.
SA1982.124B, 125, 126A Peter Thomson with Brian Lambie, EL.
SA1982.126B Sandy Robertson with Brian Lambie, EL.
SA1984.030 Harry Fox with Bob Pringle, EL.
SA1984.031 Mrs Annie Paterson, EL.
SA1984.032 Walter Culbertson, EL.
SA1984.033 Walter Culbertson and Tom Ovens, EL.
SA1984.035 Wat Ramage, EL.
SA1993.072 David Kerr with his wife, Ann Kerr, EL with Audrey Bain.
SA1996.065 Michael Crosby with his wife, Edith Crosby, EL with Laurie Romanosky.
SA1998.100 Ian Hunter, EL with Kerry Cardell.
SA2001.025 Mrs Sheila Duffy, *née* Harris, EL with Kirsten Anderson, Terry Gunnell, Angela McCulloch, Andrew Morrison and Emma Vickerstaff.
SA2003.060 William B. Brown, EL with Ian MacKenzie and Susanna Leveghi.
VD004 Kippen
VD008 Morebattle

Electronic resources

Tobar an Dualchais/Kist o' Riches
<http://www.tobarandualchais.co.uk/>   [accessed May 2011]

SCRAN
<http://www.scran.ac.uk/>   [accessed May 2011]

Folk Play Research
<http://www.folkplay.info/>   [accessed May 2011]

Master Mummers
<http://mastermummers.org/>   [accessed May 2011]

GLOSSARY

This selective list contains terms found in the text that may require explanation:

aa: all
aatogether: altogether
ahint: behind
apiece: each
auld: old
awfie: awfully, very
aye: yes, always
bairn, bairnie: child
bawbee: ha'penny
besom: broom
bine: washing-tub
bit: bit of
blather: bladder
blethering: talking nonsense
blinkin: blind in one eye
bobby: policeman
bonnie: pretty
bunnet: bonnet
burn: stream
caa: call
came away: produced
cannae: cannot
cauld: cold
chapping: knocking
claes: clothes
coo: cow
copper: penny
curdie: very small coin
dae: do
deid: dead
didna, didnae: did not
dinna: do not
divot: turf
divvy: dividend, portion
done: did
dooking: bobbing
duik: duck
dunt: blow
een: at een, in the evening
efter: after
faa: fall
fae: from
false faces: masks covering the face
ficht: fight
finnan haddies: smoked haddocks
first-footing: visiting houses after midnight at New Year
flair: floor
focht: fought
forrit: forward
gaes: goes
gaither: gather
gang: go
gaun: going
gear: property
gey: very
gie: give
grumble: complaining person
guddle: grope
guid: good
guidman: husband, master of the house
guiser, guisart: person taking part in seasonal house-visiting in disguise
guising, guisartin: seasonal house-visiting by people in disguise

GLOSSARY

haud: hold
heid: head
hing: hang
hivna: have not
Hogmanay: last evening of the year; a gift given at this time
inky pinky: small beer
intae: into
intil: unto, to
ither: other
ken: know
kin: kind
kinda, kina: kind of
laddie: boy
lassie: girl
lum: chimney
lum hat: top hat
lundering: scolding
ma: my
masel: myself
mind: remember
mines: mine
muckle: great, big
nae: no
no: not
ower: over
peenytick, pinnytick: game in which a small object is made to tap at a window
penny geggies: travelling players
pickle: little
pinnie: pin-leg, wooden leg
pinny: pinafore, apron
pooch: pouch, pocket
presses: cupboards
reek: smoke
richt: right
road: way
scoff: eat
shake yer feathers: shake up the feathers of your feather-bed
shin: shoes

siguisin: Biggar term for seasonal house-visiting by people in disguise
skip: peak or brim of a cap or bonnet
skuil: school
sleek: sneak
smokie: unsplit smoked haddock
snuff: sniff
sortie: sort of
spurtle: stick for stirring porridge
sugarallie: liquorice
sugarallie water: water with liquorice dissolved in it
tae: to
tanner: sixpence
tatties: potatoes
tee: to
they: these
thon: that
thrupenny bit: coin worth three pence
thruppence: three pence
tile hat: top hat
tuppence: two pence
turn: party piece
twa, twae: two
wan: one
wasnae: was not
wee: little
werena: were not
wha, whae: who
whiles: sometimes
wi: with
wife: woman
wir: our
wirsel: ourselves
wis: was
wisna, wisnae: was not
wouldna: would not
ye: you
ye's: you would
yer: your
yin, yun: one
yon: that